THE ATID BIBLIOGRAPHY

THE

ATID

BIBLIOGRAPHY

A Resource for the
Questioning Jew

UNITED SYNAGOGUE OF AMERICA
Department of Youth Activities
New York

ACKNOWLEDGEMENTS

The Editor would like to acknowledge the assistance of Ernest Weiss, who assisted with the original manuscript; Dr. Menachem Schmelzer and Rabbi Neil Gillman, who proofread the manuscript and advised so skillfully; Sandy Levin and Susan Unger, who typed the manuscript; and Melinda Kieffer and Margo Sack, who coordinated the project.

Thanks also go to the following individuals who allowed use of their photographs for the covers: Sandy Silverstein and Jules Gutin of the Department of Youth Activities, United Synagogue of America; and Marjorie Wyler of the Public Information Office of The Jewish Theological Seminary of America.

DEDICATION

The publication of the ATID BIBLIOGRAPHY could not have been possible without the unfailing dedication and determined efforts by the Editor. Readers of this bibliography are indeed indebted to Bertie Schwartz, who referred to her voluntary efforts as a "labor of love." It is because of her devotion to increasing Judaic knowledge that the Jewish community will continue to grow from strength to strength.

It is unfortunate that Bertie could not witness the fulfillment of her labors on this publication. On September 22, 1976, she was taken from our midst, leaving an empty void among her family, friends and colleagues.

BERTIE SCHWARTZ ז"ל

A woman of valor who can find?
She is more precious than rubies.

(Proverbs 31:10)

THE ATID BIBLIOGRAPHY

The ATID BIBLIOGRAPHY is intended to offer guidance in reading, study and education to those students and devotees, both serious and cursory, who are seeking information about the vast field of knowledge and experience known as Judaica.

Annotations are written with an attempt to be clear and concise, containing data that should aid in the ease of title selection. The reader will find useful the division of subject categories, and the cross-indexing of authors and titles to those subjects.

The BIBLIOGRAPHY is a publication of ATID, the college-age program of the National Youth Commission of the United Synagogue of America.

EDITOR

Bertie Schwartz

EDITORIAL ASSISTANTS

Melinda M. Kieffer
Margo Sack

Department of Youth Activities

Rabbi Paul Freedman
Robert J. Leifert
Sandy Silverstein
Jules A. Gutin
Karen Legman Segal
Margo Sack
Rabbi Stephen Garfinkel

Central Youth Commission

Seymour Goldberg, Chairman
Rabbi Simon Glustrom, ATID Chairman

CONTENTS

INTRODUCTION

One of the indications of a healthy and vigorous Jewish community is its interest in matters Jewish. The American Jewish community can be proud of the ever-increasing number of Judaica publications in so many fields. Books on Jewish religion, history, literature, philosophy and sociology are appearing on the American book market, some in hard cover, much in paperback. The classics of our heritage are becoming available in fine English translations, and solid scholarly studies on many aspects of the Jewish past and present can now be found on the shelves of the bookstores and libraries. As a matter of fact, there is now at our disposal a tremendous wealth of English language Judaica. The reader and the student sometimes are bewildered by these riches.

It is, therefore, with great joy and gratefulness that the present bibliography is welcomed. This new bibliography offers expert and reliable guidance through the maze of American Judaica. An intelligent subject division, accompanied by concise and relevant annotations, as well as information on the price and availability of each title, will give into the hands of the student and lay reader a very handy, most practical and eminently useful reference guide.

The Department of Youth Activities of the United Synagogue of America is to be congratulated on sponsoring and completing such a valuable and worthwhile project.

DR. MENAHEM SCHMELZER
Head Librarian
The Jewish Theological Seminary of America

ANTI-SEMITISM

(See also: Russian Jewry, Holocaust, Judaism & Christianity)

ABEL, ERNEST. *The Roots of Anti-Semitism.* The social, political, economic and religious factors that combine to single out the Jews as a people apart. Fairleigh Dickinson U., 1974, $10.00.

ALLPORT, GORDON. *The Nature of Prejudice.* Prejudice: roots in individual psychology, history, social structure and as expressed in interpersonal and societal relations. Anchor, 1958, $2.95.

ARENDT, HANNAH. *Anti-Semitism.* An interpretation of modern anti-Semitism. The modern state and its totalitarian potential. Harcourt Brace Jovanovich, 1973, $4.95 paperback.

BERNSTEIN, HERMAN. *The Truth About the Protocols of Zion.* The full story behind the notorious publication which was first published in Russia in 1903. Ktav, 1975, revised edition, $19.95.

BROUN, HEYWOOD, and BRITT, GEORGE. *Christians Only: A Study in Prejudice.* A reprint of the 1931 edition, detailing anti-Jewish practices in American intellectual life, education, society, jobs. DaCapo Press, 1975, $12.50.

COHEN, NAOMI W. *Not Free to Desist: The American-Jewish Committee, 1906-1966.* A history of the defense organization and its involvement in Jewish social and cultural life in the United States and abroad. Jewish Publication Society, 1972, $7.50.

COHN, NORMAN. *Warrant for Genocide: The Myth of the Jewish World Conspiracy and the Protocols of the Elders of Zion.* An analysis of the origins and use of the "protocols of the Elders of Zion," the most persistent canard used by anti-Semites. Harper-Torch, 1969, $2.45 paperback.

FORSTER, ARNOLD; EPSTEIN, BENJAMIN R.; and VORSPAN, ALBERT. *The New Anti-Semitism.* Results of a three-year study documenting the "resuscitation" of anti-Semitic attitudes and behavior throughout the world. McGraw-Hill, 1974, $7.95.

GLASSMAN, BERNARD. *Anti-Semitism Without Jews: Images of Jews in*

England, 1290-1700. The persistence of anti-Semitic attitudes during the 400-year period when there were no Jewish communities in England. Wayne State University Press, 1975, $11.95.

GLOCK, CHARLES Y., et al. *Adolescent Prejudice.* A study of Anti-Semitism and other forms of prejudice found in the young people of contemporary America. Harper & Row, 1975, $12.50.

——————————, and STARK, RODNEY. *Christian Beliefs and Anti-Semitism: A Scientific Study of the Ways in Which the Teachings of Christian Churches Shape American Attitudes towards the Jews.* Harper & Row, 1969, $1.95 paperback.

HAY, MALCOLM. *Thy Brother's Blood: The Pressure of Christendom on the People of Israel for 1900 Years.* One of the best histories of its kind. Hart, 1975, $4.95.

LAWRENCE, GUNTHER. *Three Million More?* Based on first-hand observations and interviews as well as extensive files of Jewish Conference on Soviet Jewry, this is an in-depth report on the oppression of the three million Jews in the Soviet Union. Tower, 1970, $.95 paperback. Out of print.

LITTELL, FRANKLIN H. *The Crucifixion of the Jews.* The avoidance of the subject of the holocaust in contemporary Christian schools and pulpits. Harper & Row, 1976, $7.95.

PARKES, JAMES. *Anti-Semitism: A Concise World History.* Covers the period from the 1870's to the 1960's. Quadrangle QP-213, 1969, $2.65 paperback.

PINSON, KOPPEL, ed. *Essays on Anti-Semitism.* Scholarly essays dealing with various periods of Jewish history. Ktav, 1973, $15.00.

POLIAKOV, LEON. *The History of Anti-Semitism.* Vol. I: From the Time of Christ to the Period of the Court Jews. Vanguard, 1964, $10.00 cloth; Schocken Books, $3.95 paperback; Vol. II: From Mohammed to the Marranos. Vanguard, 1973, $15.00; Vol. III: From Voltaire to Wagner. Vanguard, 1976, $15.00.

RUBIN, RONALD I. *The Unredeemed: Anti-Semitism in the Soviet Union.* Foreword by Abraham J. Heschel. Articles drawn from American, English, Russian, Austrian and Swiss sources. Contains much of the material which until now has been hidden in magazine articles. Quadrangle/Harper, 1975, $10.95.

RUETHER, ROSEMARY R. *Faith and Fratricide.* Evidence of the Christian origins of anti-Semitism in the New Testament. Seabury, 1975, $8.95.

RUNES, DAGOBERT. *Let My People Live.* How the anti-Jewish passages in the New Testament were exploited by Church and Christendom to promote Jew-hatred and murder. Philosophical Library, 1975, $5.00.

SAMUEL, MAURICE. *The Second Crucifixion.* In telling the story of the tiny Jewish sect which clashed with the church fathers, Mr. Samuel lays bare some of the historic roots of anti-Semitism which plague us to this day. Alfred A. Knopf. Out of print.

SARTRE, JEAN-PAUL. *Anti-Semite and Jew.* A subjective analysis of the course of modern anti-Semitism. Schocken Books, 1948, $2.45.

SCHORSCH, ISMAR. *Jewish Reactions to German Anti-Semitism: 1870-1914.* A systematic attempt to provide a comprehensive examination of the variety of organized responses by different segments of the German Jewish community to anti-Semitism before the first World War. A detailed portrayal of the radical shift in strategy: away from reliance on silence, Christian spokesmen and Jewish courtiers toward overt affirmation of Jewishness in the form of a mass organization committed to public self-defense. Columbia Univ. Press, 1972, $10.00.

SELZNICK, GERTRUDE, and STEINBERG, STEPHEN. *The Tenacity of Prejudice: Anti-Semitism in Contemporary America.* Harper & Row, 1969, $1.95 paperback.

ADAR, ZVI. *The Biblical Narrative.* An analysis of the nature of the Biblical tale and the enduring lessons that it teaches. World Zionist Organization, 1959, $2.50.

—————————. *Humanistic Values in the Bible.* An approach to teaching the Bible based upon Israeli educational methods. Reconstructionist Pres, 1967, $6.50.

AHARONI, YOHANAN. *The Land of the Bible: A Historical Geography.* Part I: the land of Israel with reference to its position in the Ancient East; Part II: factors affecting the history of settlement, place names, archaeology; Part III: historical development of the country from the proto-historic period to the time of the Persian Empire. Westminster Press, 1967, $7.95.
Related titles: BALY, DENNIS. *The Geography of the Bible* (rev. ed.). Harper & Row, 1974, $10.95; ORNI, EPHRAIM, and EFRAT, ELISHA. *Geography of Israel,* Jewish Publication Society, 1973, $10.95. Both titles more oriented toward physical geography.

AHARONI, YOHANAN, and AVI YONAH, MICHAEL. *The Macmillan Bible Atlas.* Indispensable. Historical maps with explanatory essays covering the history of ancient Israel. (See *Reference.*) Macmillan, 1968, $9.95.

ALBRIGHT, WILLIAM F. *From the Stone Age to Christianity.* The contribution made to Biblical research by the "founder" of its archaeological school. Doubleday, 1957, $1.75, paperback. Second Edition.

ALT, ALBRECHT. *Essays on Old Testament History and Religion.* A collection of essays by one of the great twentieth-century German Bible scholars. Doubleday, 1966, $1.45.

The Anchor Bible. A series of new translations, now in progress, with notes and commentaries by leading contemporary scholars, utilizing the methods and discoveries of modern Biblical research. Published so far: Genesis, Proverbs and Ecclesiastes, Job, Ezra, and Nehemiah, I and II Chronicles, Jeremiah, 2nd Isaiah, Judges. The latest volume is Ruth. Robert G. Bowling, translator and commentator. Doubleday, 1964, $8.00 (prices vary).

AUERBACH, ELIAS. *Moses.* One of the classics of Biblical scholarship, now available in English. Wayne State University Press, 1975, $13.95.

AUERBACH, ERICH. *Mimesis: The Representation of Reality in Western Literature.* The first essay compares the literary character of the Bible and Homeric epic narratives as reflections of the Jewish and Greek world views. Princeton Univ. Press, 1953, $3.45.

BARTEL, ROLAND; ACKERMAN, JAMES; and WARSAW, THAYER S. *Biblical Images in Literature.* Analyses of the work of famous writers stressing the use of Biblical motifs in world literature. Abingdon Press, 1975, $10.00.

BERCOVICI, MYRNA. *Prophecy.* Quotations from the prophets illuminated by photographs from the Warsaw Ghetto, the concentration camps, Mi Lai, Kent State, etc. Tarcher/Hawthorn, 1975, $3.95 paperback.

BERKOVITS, ELIEZER. *Man and God: Studies in Biblical Theology.* Clarifies specific Biblical concepts such as justice, holiness, truth, etc. Wayne State Univ. Press, 1969, $12.50.

BICKERMAN, ELIAS. *Four Strange Books of the Bible.* Essays by the renowned scholar on Jonah, Daniel, Kohelet, and Esther. Schocken, 1968, $7.50.

BRAUDE, WILLIAM G. *Midrash on Psalms* (Midrash Tehellim). Yale Univ. Press, 1959, $20.00, two-volume set.

BRIGHT, JOHN. *History of Israel.* Westminster Press, second edition, 1972, $10.95.

BUBER, MARTIN. *Good and Evil.* Biblical interpretations: 1) several Psalms, the Tree of Knowledge, Cain and Abel; 2) the mythological origins of good and evil in the ancient world. Scribner's, 1953, $2.45, paperback.

—————————. *Moses: The Revelation and the Covenant.* A work of consummate Biblical scholarship. Harper & Row, 1958, $2.95 paperback.

——————. *On the Bible.* Eighteen studies. Schocken Books, $5.95.

——————. *The Prophetic Faith.* An existential interpretation of Biblical religion as confrontation between God and man. Harper and Row, 1960, $2.25.

CAMPBELL, EDWARD, JR., and FREEDMAN, DAVID N. *The Biblical Archaeologist Reader.* Vol. 3. Essays by prominent archaeologists, shedding new light on Biblical texts. Doubleday, 1970, $2.45 paperback. Volumes 1 and 2, also Doubleday.

CASSUTO, UMBERTO. *From Adam to Noah; From Noah to Abraham; Exodus.* Three volumes of Bible commentary. Ideas reflect those of Ibn Ezra. Magnes Press, Jerusalem, 1961.

——————. *The Documentary Hypothesis.* An account and exploration of the hypothesis that the Biblical narrative is composed of several different documents or source materials that have become identified as J.E.P.D. Magnes Press, Jerusalem, 1961.

DAITCHES, DAVID. *Moses, the Man and His Vision.* The Biblical biography of the towering religious genius is illuminated, and confirmed by modern archaeological, anthropological, historical and linguistic evidence. A popular presentation. Praeger Publishers, $19.95.

DEVAUX, ROLAND. *Ancient Israel: Its Life and Institutions.* History of religious and social institutions of ancient Israel. McGraw-Hill, 1965, two volumes, $2.95 each, paperback.

——————. *The Bible and the Ancient Near East.* Doubleday, 1971, $6.95.

DORIA, CHARLES, and LENOWITZ, HARRIS. *Origins: Creation Texts from the Ancient Mediterranean.* Selections drawn from Mesopotamian, Canaanite, Phoenician, Gnostic, Hebraic, and Dionysian sources from 2000 BCE to 200 CE. Doubleday Anchor AO-141, 1976, $3.95.

EICHRODT, WALTHER. *Man in the Old Testament.* An analysis of the

Biblical view of man. Allenson, 1951, $6.95 hardbound; $3.85 paperback.

—————————. *Theology of the Old Testament*. Translated by J. Baker. Westminster Press, Vol. I, 1961, $8.50; Vol. II, $7.95.

EISSFELDT, OTTO. *The Old Testament: An Introduction*. A comprehensive analysis of every book in the Tanach and of the Biblical historiography, legal theory, etc. A massive work of German scholarship. Standard reference. Harper & Row, 1965, $11.00.
Related titles: CESTERLY, W. O. E., and ROBINSON, THEODORE. *An Introduction to the Books of the Old Testament*. Meridian, paperback; DRIVER, S. R. *An Introduction to the Literature of the Old Testament*. Meridian, paperback; PFEIFFER, ROBERT H. *Introduction to the Old Testament*. Harper & Row.

Five Megilloth and the Book of Jonah. With Introductory Essays by H. L. Ginsberg. Jewish Publication Society, 1969, $5.00.

GINZBERG, LOUIS. *Legends of the Bible*. A one-volume selection from the author's *Legends of the Jews*, culls the principal Biblical legends from a wide variety of literary sources. Jewish Publication Society, 1956, $7.95.

GLATZER, NAHUM N., ed. *The Dimensions of Job*. Analytical essays on the aspects of the Book of Job as seen from the Jewish, Christian and philosophical points of view. Schocken Books, 1969, $7.95 hardbound; $3.95 paperback.

GOLDMAN, ALEX J. *Power of the Bible*. Rabbi Goldman summarizes the heart of the Bible and emphasizes those aspects which are eminently significant today. Fountainhead Publ., 1972, $12.00.

GORDIS, ROBERT. *Kohelet: The Man and His World*. A study of Ecclesiastes' Hebrew text with a new translation, interpretation and commentary. A thorough literary, stylistic, and philosophical analysis against the background of Hebrew, Greek, and Near Eastern wisdom literature. Schocken Books, 1968, $3.95.

—————————————. *Poets, Prophets and Sages: Essays in Biblical Interpretation.* Indiana University Press, 1971, $15.00.

HERTZ, JOSEPH H., ed. *The Pentateuch and Haftorahs.* Hebrew text and commentary. Guide to the weekly portions of the Scriptures. Soncino, 1960, $12.00.

HESCHEL, ABRAHAM JOSHUA. *The Prophets.* A clear analysis of the major prophets and an exposition of the differences that separate their thinking from that of other religions. Jewish Publication Society, 1962, $6.00. Harper Torch, TB 1421, $2.95; TB 1557, $3.25.

HILLERS, DELBERT R. *Covenant: The History of a Biblical Idea.* The concept of Covenant as presented in the Bible, and as held by surrounding peoples. Johns Hopkins, 1969, $7.00 cloth; $1.95 paperback.

The Holy Scriptures According to the Masoretic Text. A standard English translation of the entire Bible. Hebrew and English in parallel columns. Jewish Publication Society, 1955 ed., $12.50, two volumes.

Isaiah: A New Translation. Original drawings by Chaim Gross. Jewish Publication Society, 1973, $12.50. Smaller edition without drawings, $4.00.

JACOBSON, B. S. *Meditations on the Torah.* Discusses themes for weekly portions of Torah. Sinai, 1969, $8.00.

Jeremiah: A New Translation. With woodcuts by Nikos Stavroulakis. Jewish Publication Society, 1975, $12.50.

KADUSHIN, MAX. *A Conceptual Approach to the Mekilta: A Basic Text for the Study of the Midrash.* Rabbinic concepts from the text of the Bible. Jonathan David, 1969, $6.95.

KATZ, ELIEZER. *A Classified Concordance to the Torah in Its Various Subjects.* English-Hebrew text. Jerusalem, 1964, $1.75.

KAUFMANN, YEHEZKEL. *The Religion of Israel From Its Beginnings to the Babylonian Exile.* An abridgement, a theory of the historical development and distinctive characteristics of Biblical religion, by one of the leading Biblical scholars of our day. A major work, for the attention of the serious student. Schocken Books, $4.95 paperback. Also: *Religion of Israel.* University of Chicago, $12.50.

—————————. Translated by C. W. Efroymson. *The Babylonian Captivity and Deutero-Isaiah: The History of the Religion of Israel,* Vol. IV. U.A.H.C., 1970, $8.75.

KELLER, WERNER. *The Bible as History.* The historical foundations of the Bible and the Gospels brought to light by the evidence gathered from archaeologists, geologists, biologists, astronomers, and physicists. Apollo Editions, 1969, $3.50; Bantam, $1.95 paperback.

KENYON, KATHLEEN. *Royal Cities of the Old Testament.* An archaeological perspective on the history and development of Jerusalem, Hazor, Gezer, Megiddo, and Samaria. Schocken Books, 1970, $4.50 paperback.

LANDAY, JERRY M. *Silent Cities, Sacred Stones.* Well written account of archaeological discoveries in Israel. Many pictures. McCall Books, 1971, $14.95.

LEIBOWITZ, NECHAMA. *Studies in the Book of Genesis.* Seven years of courses in Chumash given by one of Israel's foremost teachers. Makes use of classical and modern Bible commentaries. World Zionist Organization, 1974, $8.50.

—————————. *Shemot.* Two volumes, World Zionist Organization, 1976, $16.00.

—————————. *Studies in the Weekly Sidra.* Translated by Aryeh Newman. Excellent study guide. Department for Torah Education and Culture, World Zionist Organization, 1955, $3.00.

LEVINE, MOSHE. *The Tabernacle.* A detailed description aided by 30 color plates follows the Torah verse by verse, in a reconstruction of the desert Mishkan. Soncino Press, 1969, $35.00.

MANDELKERN, SOLOMON. *Concordance on the Bible.* Hebrew. Excellent reference. Schocken, $22.00.

MATEK, ORD. *The Bible Through Stamps.* An anthology of stamps from many lands accompanied by philatelic and Biblical historical commentary. Ktav, 1974, $7.50.

MAZAR, BENJAMIN, and AVI YONAH, MICHAEL, general editors. *A World History of the Jewish People.* Collections of scholarly essays by outstanding authorities. Titles published on the Bible: *The Dawn of History,* E. A. Speiser, editor, $20.00; *The Patriarchs,* Benjamin Mazar, editor, $20.00; *Judges,* Benjamin Mazar, editor, $20.00. Rutgers University Press. (See also *Hellenism and Middle Ages.*)

MUILENBURG, JAMES. *The Way of Israel: Biblical Faith and Ethics.* A survey of Biblical faith and ethics. Recommended for readability and breadth of perspective. Harper & Row, 1965, $1.75 paperback.

NACHMAN, MOSHE BEN. *Commentary on the Torah.* Translated and edited by Rabbi Dr. Charles Chavel. Available: Genesis to Numbers. Deuteronomy scheduled 1977. Shilo Publishing House, 1971-1975, $13.50 per volume.

NEHER, ANDRE. *The Prophetic Existence.* An examination of the form and substance of prophecy and of the men in whom word and vision became a category of revelation. One of the best books in the field. A. S. Barnes, 1969, $10.00.

Notes on the New Translation of the Torah, edited by Harry Orlinsky. Jewish Publication Society, 1970, $6.00.

NOTH, MARTIN. *The History of Israel.* Harper & Row, 1958.

PEARLMAN, MOSHE. *The First Days of Israel: In the Footsteps of Moses.* A lavishly illustrated book tracing the life of Moses and Israel from Egypt to settlement in Canaan. T. Y. Crowell, 1973, $19.95.

——————. *In the Footsteps of the Prophets.* The continuation of the story. T. Y. Crowell, 1975, $19.95.

PLAUT, W. GUNTHER. *The Torah: A Modern Commentary. Vol. I, Genesis.* The first of a projected five-volume translation which includes the Hebrew text and Rabbinic and scholarly commentaries. U.A.H.C., 1974, $12.50 hardbound; $7.95 paperback.

PRITCHARD, JAMES. *The Ancient Near East.* (See listing under *History: Ancient and Archaeology.*)

Psalms, A New Translation. Jewish Publication Society, 1972, $6.00.

ROBINSON, H. WHEELER. *Inspiration and Revelation in the Old Testament.* Introductory lectures to Biblical theology. Oxford University Press, 1946, $4.25 cloth; $2.25 paperback.

ROSENBAUM, M., and SILBERMANN, A. M., eds. & trans. *Pentateuch with Rashi.* Rashi's complete commentary is given in square Hebrew vowelled type (not "Rashi" script), with full English translation and exhaustive notes that make it thoroughly understandable. Hebrew Publishing Company, 5 volumes, $30.00.

SAMUEL, EDITH, ed. *In the Beginning Love: Dialogues on the Bible Between Mark Van Doren and Maurice Samuel.* Fifteen dialogues on the Bible that were featured on the summer programs of "The Eternal Light." Witty, spontaneous, the dialogues speak not only of "love" in the Bible, but of a great love of the Bible. John Day, 1973, $8.95.

SAMUEL, MAURICE. *Certain People of the Book.* A personal encounter with certain Biblical personalities. The interpretations are witty, intelligent, and absolutely true to the Text. Extremely pleasant, personal reading. Alfred A. Knopf, 1955, $5.95.

SANDERS, PAUL S. *Twentieth Century Interpretations of the Book of Job.* A collection of critical essays. Prentice-Hall/Spectrum, 1968, $4.95.

SANDMEL, SAMUEL. *Old Testament Issues.* Scholarly essays; especially recommended are the contributions of G. Ernest Wright and Robert Gordis. Harper & Row, 1968, $3.50.

SARNA, NAHUM M. *Understanding Genesis: The Heritage of Biblical Israel.*

A readable, thorough introduction to a scholarly understanding of Genesis. Schocken Books, $2.95 paperback. Also available: *Genesis: Teacher's Guide*, $6.50; *Genesis: Student's Guide*, Part I, $3.95; Part II, $4.95. Melton Research Center, 1970.

SCOTT, R. B. Y. *The Relevance of the Prophets.* A positive analysis useful as background material for an actual reading-teaching of Nevi'im. Macmillan, 1969, $2.45 paperback.

SNAITH, NORMAN. *Distinctive Ideas of the Old Testament.* These are explained in terms of key words such as *q-d-sh,* ruach, tsedaqah, and others. Schocken Books, 1964, $2.25 paperback.

The Soncino Books of the Bible. The Hebrew texts, with parallel translations and selections in English from the classical Rabbinic commentaries. Soncino Press, 1947, fourteen volumes, $82.00 complete set; $6.75 each volume except Chumash—$11.75.

SPEISER, E. A. *Oriental and Biblical Studies: Collected Writings of E. A. Speiser,* J. J. Finkelstein, Moshe Greenberg. University of Pennsylvania, 1967, $12.00.

The Torah, The Five Books of Moses. A new translation by a committee of world famous scholars. Jewish Publication Society, 1962, $6.00.

VON RAD, GERHARD. *Wisdom in Israel.* What Wisdom is saying, and its relationship to the rest of Israelite faith. A full length study of the Biblical and non-Biblical literary genre. Abingdon Press, $12.95.

—————————. *Genesis, A Commentary.* One of the modern classical commentaries. Westminster, 1973, $8.50.

—————————. *The Message of the Prophets.* The message of each prophet is examined individually, against the background of his time, and with regard to his significance for ours. Harper & Row, 1972, $3.95 paperback.

—————————. *Old Testament Theology.* Two volumes. Harper & Row, 1962-65, Vol. I $9.00; Vol. II $8.00.

WEINBERG, NORBERT. *The Essential Torah.* A comprehensive review of the Torah and Haftorah with selected notes from classical commentaries. Bloch, 1974, $8.95.

WELLHAUSEN, JULIUS. *Prolegomena to the History of Ancient Israel.* The classic statement of nineteenth-century Higher Biblical Criticism which formed the basis of the modern re-examination of the Bible. Peter Smith, 1957, $6.75.

BIOGRAPHY AND AUTOBIOGRAPHY

AGUS, JACOB B. *High Priest of Rebirth: The Life, Times and Thought of Rabbi Abraham Isaac Kook.* Rabbi Kook's faith in the Divine, thrust toward perfection, his mystical conception of Zionism, and his generous, outgoing humanism. Bloch, 1972, $6.95.

ALEICHEM, SHOLOM. *The Great Fair: Scenes from My Childhood.* An autobiographical novel of the author's experiences as a growing boy in a small town in Russia. Noonday, 1970, $1.45 paperback.

ALTMANN, ALEXANDER. *Moses Mendelsohn: A Biographical Study.* A comprehensive treatment of the famous figure of the Jewish German Enlightenment. University of Alabama Press, 1973, $15.00.

ANTIN, MARY. *The Promised Land.* A re-issue with a new foreword by Oscar Handlin of the autobiography of an immigrant girl, first published in 1912. Houghton Mifflin, 1969, $5.95.

BAR-ZOHAR, MICHAEL. *Ben Gurion: The Armed Prophet.* Biography of the first prime minister of Israel. Prentice Hall, 1968, $7.95.

BEIN, ALEX. *Theodore Herzl.* The classic biography of the great Zionist leader. Atheneum, 1962, $4.75 paperback.

BENTWICH, NORMAN. *Solomon Schechter: A Biography.* The life and scholarly work of the former president of the Jewish Theological Seminary. Burning Bush Press, 1964, $5.00.

————. *For Zion's Sake: A Biography of Judah I. Magnes.* The eminent American Jewish leader, Zionist, first chancellor and first president of the Hebrew University, Jerusalem. Jewish Publication Society, 1954. Out of print.

BERMANT, CHAIM. *The Cousinhood.* An account of the English Jewish aristocracy: the Rothschilds, Sassons, Goldsmids, Montefiores, Samuels, Cohens, and other interlocking families. Macmillan, 1972, $10.95.

CAHAN, ABRAHAM. *The Education of Abraham Cahan.* Autobiography of the man who founded and edited the Yiddish newspaper, "The

Forward." Jewish Publication Society, 1969, $7.50.

COWLES, VIRGINIA. *The Rothschilds: Family of Fortune.* A lavishly illustrated history of the great family, written with verve and scholarship. Knopf, 1973, $17.50.
Related title: *The Rothschilds, A Family Portrait.* Frederic Morton.
Illus. Atheneum, 1962, $6.95; Fawcett World, 1970, $9.95.

DAVID, JAY, ed. *Growing Up Jewish.* Twenty-five Jews relive their child-
hoods in Europe, America, and Israel. Their experiences span four
centuries and present Jewish history in an intensely personal way.
Pocket Books, 1970, $.95.

ELON, AMOS. *Herzl.* Biography of the Zionist visionary. Holt, Rinehart
and Winston, 1975, $15.00.

FARRER, DAVID. *The Warburgs.* The story of an extraordinary family,
ranking with the Rockefellers and Rothschilds, but before this
biography, almost unknown to the general public. Stein & Day,
1974, $8.95.

FEUCHTWANGER, LION. *Josephus.* A historical novel based upon the
life of the Jewish historian, author of the book entitled *The Jewish
War.* Atheneum, 1972, $4.95 paperback.

FINKELSTEIN, LOUIS. *Akiba: Scholar, Saint and Martyr.* Memorable
biography of one of the greatest of the Rabbinic teachers. Jewish
Publication Society, Atheneum, 1970, $3.25.

GINZBERG, ELI. *Keeper of the Law: Louis Ginzberg.* A biography of Professor
Louis Ginzberg. A devoted tribute paid by a son to his father and an
insight into the life of a great scholar and teacher. Jewish Publication
Society, 1966, $6.00.

GLATZER, NAHUM N., ed. *Franz Rosenzweig: His Life and Thought.*
Biography based on letters, diaries, and a cross section of his Jewish
and philosophical writings. Schocken, 1961, $3.95 paperback,
2nd ed., revised.

BIOGRAPHY AND AUTOBIOGRAPHY

GLUCKEL OF HAMELIN. *Her Autobiography.* The story of an energetic, intelligent, vital woman. Her memoirs have been recognized as a primary source for research into the life and customs of Jews in 17th century Germany. Thomas Yoseloff, $5.95. Out of print.

GOLDMANN, NAHUM. *The Autobiography of Nahum Goldmann: 60 Years of Jewish Life.* Story of one of the most influential Jewish communal leaders. Holt, Rinehart & Winston, 1969, $7.95.

HELLER, JAMES G. *Isaac Meyer Wise: His Life, Work and Thought.* A definitive study of the father of Reform Judaism in America. U.A.H.C., 1965, $10.00.

KALB, MARVIN, and KALB, BERNARD. *Kissinger.* A portrait of the U.S. Secretary of State. Dell Books, 1974, $1.95 paperback.

LANDAU, DAVID. *Kissinger: The Uses of Power.* An intellectual portrait of the U.S. Secretary of State. Apollo, 1972, $2.95 paperback.

LEVIN, SHMARYA. *Forward From Exile: The Autobiography of Shmarya Levin.* The life of the great Russian Zionist leader is also a record and an evocation of personalities active in the early Zionist movement. Jewish Publication Society, 1967, $7.50.

LOWENTHAL, MARVIN, ed. *The Diaries of Theodore Herzl.* Copious excerpts from the diaries of the father of the Jewish State. Grosset & Dunlap, 1965, $2.95.

MALTER, HENRY. *Saadya Gaon: His Life and Works.* The classic treatment of Saadya and his works in readable, well-documented fashion. Hermon, 1969, $10.00.

MANN, PEGGY. *Golda: The Life of Israel's Prime Minister.* Pocket Books, 1973, $1.25 paperback.

MASTERS, ANTHONY. *Summer That Bled: The Biography of Hannah Senesh.* (See listing under *Holocaust.*)

MEIR, GOLDA. *My Life.* A forceful autobiography intertwining personal history with the story of the State of Israel. Putnam, 1975, $12.50.

NETANYAHU, BEN ZION. *Don Isaac Abravanel: Statesman and Philosopher.* The famous statesman, financier, philosopher and Bible commentator whose illustrious career and magnificent intellect symbolize the Golden Age and the tragic end of the Spanish Jewish community. Jewish Publication Society, 1968, $5.00.

NOVECK, SIMON, ed. *Great Jewish Personalities in Ancient and Medieval Times. Great Jewish Personalities in Modern Times. Great Jewish Thinkers in the Twentieth Century.* Biographies written by scholarly authorities. B'nai B'rith Adult Education Dept., 1959-1963, $5.95 cloth, $3.95 paperback, each volume. Other titles in this series listed under: *Theology and Philosophy.*

PERETZ, I. L. *My Memoirs.* Translated by Fred Goldberg. A personal history and vivid portrait of a people in abject poverty and misery, deprived by czarist laws of the most elementary civil rights. Citadel Press, 1965, $3.50.

SIMON, LEON. *Ahad Ha'am: A Biography.* Special attention is focused on the content, motivation, and influence of his essays. Jewish Publication Society, 1960, $4.50.

——————. *Selected Essays of Ahad Ha'am.* Atheneum, 1970, $3.95.

SYRKIN, MARIE, ed. *A Land of Our Own: An Oral Autobiography. Golda Meir.* A unique volume containing the "autobiographical statement" of the former Prime Minister on Zionism, Israel and her own life." An in-depth portrait of an extraordinary woman. Putnam, 1973, $6.95.

TEVETH, SHABTAI. *Moshe Dayan: The Soldier, the Man, the Legend.* Houghton-Mifflin, 1973, $8.95.

VOSS, CARL HERMANN, ed. *Stephen S. Wise: Servant of the People.* Collection of letters by Wise on Zionism, Palestine, Liberal Judaism, and social reform. Jewish Publication Society, 1969, $5.50.

WAIFE-GOLDBERG, MARIE. *My Father, Sholom Aleichem.* Biography of the famous Jewish humorist, written by his daughter. Schocken, 1971, $3.45.

WEISGAL, MEYER, general editor. *The Letters and Papers of Chaim Weizmann.* Israel Universities Press, Jerusalem, 1973, seven volumes, I-IV, $12.50 each; V-VII $17.50 each.

WEIZMANN, CHAIM. *Trial and Error: The Autobiography of Chaim Weizmann.* (Reprint of 1949 edition.) Greenwood, 1972, $7.75 cloth; Schocken, 1966, $3.95 paperback.

YELLIN, DAVID, and ABRAHAMS, ISRAEL. *Maimonides: His Life and Works.* Hermon Press, 1973, $7.95.

CLASSICS IN TRANSLATION

ALBO, JOSEPH. *Sefer Ha-Ikkarim: Book of Principles.* Ed. by Isaac Husik. Critically edited on the basis of manuscripts and old editions and provided with a translation and notes. Jewish Publication Society, 1929, four volumes. Out of print.

AL-HARIZI, JUDAH. *The Tahkemoni of Judah al-Harizi.* Edited by Victor Reichert. Work of a 13th century Spanish-Jewish poet. Bloch, 1975, Vol. 1, $10; Vol. 2, $14.95.

BAHYA BEN-JOSEPH IBN PAKUKA. *Book of Direction to the Duties of the Heart* (Chovoth Halevavoth). Translated by Moses Hyamson. One of the classics of earliest Musar literature. Feldheim, 1970, $12.50, two volumes.

BLACKMAN, PHILIP, ed. *The Mishnah.* This classical storehouse of knowledge of the Oral Law is given with Hebrew text vocalized (menukad), rendered into English, and thoroughly annotated.Judaica, 1963-1964, $40.00.

BRAUDE, WILLIAM G., trans. *Pesikta de Rab-Kahana.* Discourses for Sabbath and festival days. Jewish Publication Society, 1975, $15.00.

——————. *Pesikta Rabbati.* Discourses for Feasts, Fasts, and Special Sabbaths. Yale University Press, 1968, $25, 2 volumes.

BUNIM, IRVING M. *Ethics from Sinai.* An eclectic, wide-ranging commentary on Pirkei Avot, drawing on the great store of classical commentaries. Feldheim, 1974, $25.00 cloth, 3 volumes, $12.50 paperback.

CHAJES, ZVI HIRSCH. *Student's Guide Through the Talmud.* Delineates the nature, extent, and authority of the Talmudic tradition in halachah and aggadah. The development of the Oral Law is made clear for the average reader. Feldheim, 1972, $7.75.

CHOFETZ CHAIM (KAHAN, ISRAEL MEIR). *Ahavath Chesed.* Translated by Leonard Oschry. Kindness required by God; a modern classic that unfolds all the ramifications of the meaning of chesed, the ways of kindness in human relations. Feldheim, 1967, $4.50.

COHEN, ARTHUR A., ed. & trans. *The Minor Tractates of the Talmud.* Redacted later than the body of the Talmud, these works, dealing more with morals and ethics than with law, are often overlooked, but they have a definite interest and importance of their own. Soncino Press, 1965-71, $25.00, 2 volumes.

COHEN, SEYMOUR, trans. *The Ways of the Righteous/Orchoth Tzadikim.* Written in the 15th century, this basic work of religious ethics has 28 chapters on such themes as modesty, charity, etc. Vocalized Hebrew text, with the translation on facing pages, accompanied by source references. Feldheim, 1974, $14.00.

DANBY, HERBERT, trans. *The Mishnah.* Reprint of 1933 edition. One volume English translation. Oxford University Press, 1974, $24.00.

ELIZUR, BARUCH, trans. & ed. *A Chapter of Talmud.* Bava Mezia IX (Perek Ha-mekabbel) with introduction, translation, commentary, and annotations. A chapter of the Babylonian Talmud with a discussion in English, tracing the various halachot from their sources to the codifiers. Treats the original text paragraph by paragraph, and gives the relevant laws from Maimonides' code. Department for Torah Education and Culture in the Diaspora, World Zionist Organization, 1974, $4.50.
Also available: *Sabbath Chapters of Talmud.* Edited by Baruch Elizur. 1972, $3.50. *Lessons in Talmud.* By Ze'ev Gold. 1956, $1.50.

EPSTEIN, ISIDORE. *The Faith of Judaism.* A foremost exponent of observant Judaism in England explains and clarifies its tenets in the light of modern thought and opinion. Soncino Press, 1960, $8.25.

FRIEDLANDER, GERALD, ed. & trans. *Pirkei de Rabbi Eliezer.* Reprint of 1916 edition. Midrashic and mythic material on the Biblical stories. Sepher-Hermon Press, 1965, $14.50.

GOLDIN, JUDAH, trans. *Aboth de Rabbi Nathan.* A rabbinic commentary on the Pirkei Avot. Schocken, 1974, $4.95 paperback.

HALEVI, AHARON. *Sefer Ha-Hinnuch (The Book of Education).* Trans. by Charles Wengrov. The classic on the 613 mitzvoth (precepts) written in 14th-century Spain for the author's young son, teaching him for every precept, the substance, requirements and procedures, and interesting and thought-provoking reasons and meanings for its observance. Feldheim, 1976, price not yet fixed.

HALEVI, JUDAH. *The Kuzari: An Argument for the Faith of Israel.* Translated by Henry Slonimsky. In the style of a Platonic dialogue, Judah Halevi presents the central teachings of Judaism: revelation, prophecy, the law, the Holy Land, and the role of the Jewish people. Schocken, 1947, $3.45 paperback.

HERFORD, R. TRAVERS. *Sayings of the Fathers.* (See listing under *Rabbinic Judaism.*)

HERTZ, JOSEPH H., ed. *Midrash Rabbah.* The complete English translation of this major work, with an introduction to each section, notes, glossary and indices. Soncino Press, 1939, $165.00, 10 volumes.

——————————. *The Zohar.* The basic text of the Jewish mystical tradition, rendered into English; with an introduction. Soncino Press, 1934, $75,000, 5 volumes.

HIRSCH, SAMSON RAPHAEL, ed. & trans. *Chapters of the Fathers.* Originally part of his work on the Siddur, Hirsch's translation and commentary on Pirkei Avot is an invaluable handbook for inspiring study. His unique outlook illuminates the ethical truths of the "Chapters." Feldheim, 1972, $3.95.

IBN CHABIB, JACOB. *En Jacob: Aggada of the Babylonian Talmud.* Trans. by S. M. Glick. Hebrew Publishing Company, 1921, $25.00, 5 volumes.

IBN EZRA, ABRAHAM. *The Commentary of Ibn Ezra on Isaiah.* Edited and translated by Michael Friedlander. The text edited from old manuscripts, with translation, notes, introduction, and index. Reprint of the first edition, London, 1873. Feldheim, 1973, $8.75.

LAUTERBACH, JACOB Z, ed. & trans. *The Mekhilta de Rabbi Ishmael.* Midrashic work commenting on the book of Exodus. Jewish Publication Society, 1933-35, reissue 1975, $13.50, 3 volumes paperback.

LEWITTES, MENDEL. *The Nature and History of Jewish Law.* Yeshiva University Press, Studies in Torah Judaism, No. 9, $3.00.

LUZZATTO, MOSES HAYYIM. *Mesillat Yesharim: The Path of the Upright.* Trans. by Shraga Silverstein. A fundamental work of Musar literature. Feldheim, 1966, $7.75.

MAIMONIDES, MOSES. *Guide for the Perplexed.* (See listing under *Theology and Philosophy.*)

——————————. *Mishneh Torah: Yad Hazakah.* Law code of Maimonides, with his philosophical introduction, the Book of Knowledge (Sefer Ha-Madda). Yale University Press, 1949-1965, 13 volumes, $15-$22.

——————————. *Moses Maimonides' Commentary on the Mishnah.* Edited and translated by Fred Rosner. Introduction to Seder Zeraim and Tractate Berakhot. The Rambam deals with the revelation at Sinai, the transmission of the Oral Torah down to Talmudic times, the nature of prophecy, and the types of law in the Mishnah. Feldheim, 1975, $7.95.

——————————. *The Commandments/Sefer Hamitzvoth.* Edited and translated by Charles Chavel. The famous work of Rambam, listing and explaining the 613 precepts of the Torah, translated from the Hebrew, with a foreword, glossary, appendices and indices. Soncino Press, 1967, $30.00, 2 volumes.

MALTER, HENRY, ed. & trans. *The Treatise of Ta'anit of the Babylonian Talmud.* Jewish Publication Society, 1967, $4.50.

NACHMAN, MOSHE BEN. *Commentary on the Torah.* (See listing under *Bible and Biblical Studies.*)

ROSENBAUM, M., and SILBERMANN, A. M., eds. & trans. *Pentateuch with Rashi.* Rashi's complete commentary is given in square Hebrew vowelled type (not "Rashi" script), with full English translation and exhaustive notes that make it thoroughly understandable. Hebrew Publishing Company, 5 volumes, $30.00.

The Soncino Hebrew-English Talmud. The Babylonian Talmud is published with the complete Hebrew-Aramaic text, with the corresponding English translation facing it page by page. Tractates Berakoth, Baba Mezia, Gittin, Baba Kamma, Kiddushin, Pesahim, Sanhedrin, Baba Batra, Ketuboth, Shabboth and Yoma have been published so far. Soncino, 1962-1974, $15.75-$39.50.

The Soncino Talmud (English Edition). The definitive Soncino translation into English, unabridged, with introduction, notes, glossary, and indices. Complete in 18 volumes. Soncino, $330.00 a set. Individual sedarim are available.

TWERSKY, ISADORE. *A Maimonides Reader.* A one-volume presentation in English of the basic writings of the Rambam, providing an excellent introduction to the whole range of Maimonidean teachings. Behrman House, 1972, $4.95 paperback.

ZALMAN, SCHNEUR (of Liadi). *Tanya (Likutei Amarim).* The classic work expounding Chassidic principles by the founder of Chabad-Chassidism. Introductions, notes, English text. Kehot, 1968-1972, 5 volumes, $1.50-$5.50.

FICTION, DRAMA, AND SHORT STORIES

AGNON, S. Y. *The Bridal Canopy.* Reb Yudel undertakes a journey through Poland to beg dowries for his three daughters. On the way he meets an assortment of characters, who have stories to exchange with his. A lovely collection of folklore in the guise of a picaresque novel, by the recipient of the 1966 Nobel Prize for Literature. Schocken, 1968, $2.95.

——————. *A Guest for the Night.* After the destruction of his home in Jerusalem by Arabs in 1929, the author returns to the Poland of his youth and witnesses the terrible decline. Schocken, 1968, $6.95.

——————. *Twenty-One Stories,* ed. by Nahum Glatzer. Each story is supplemented by a bibliographical postscript and thematic analysis. Schocken, 1970, $2.95.

ALEICHEM, SHOLOM. *Adventures of Mottel, the Cantor's Son.* The adventures of a Jewish Huckleberry Finn in Kasrilevke and New York. Collier, 1953, $1.25.

——————. *Inside Kasrilevke.* The great Jewish humorist's imaginary home town, revisited after years in the great world. Illustrated by by Ben Shahn. Schocken, 1965, $4.95; $2.25 paperback. Other titles: *The Old Country.* Crown, 1956, $1.98. *Tevye's Daughters.* Crown, 1959, $1.98.

ANGOFF, CHARLES. *Mid-Century.* This volume covers the 1950's and is the latest in Angoff's massive continuing work on American Jewish life. Also: *Bitter Spring, Sun at Noon, Winter Twilight, In the Morning Light, Journey to the Dawn, Season of Mist.* A. S. Barnes, 1973, $7.95.

BELLOW, SAUL, ed. *Great Jewish Stories.* Includes stories by Philip Roth, Isaac Bashevis Singer, Bernard Malamud, and others. Dell, 1963, $1.50 paperback.

——————. *Herzog.* Novel of an American Jew, facing life questions of the post-holocaust 20th century. Fawcett, 1969, $1.75 paperback.

BLOCKER, JOEL. *Israeli Stories.* Representative modern Hebrew stories in translation. Schocken, 1969, $1.95 paperback.

GRADE, CHAIM. *The Agunah.* Translated by Curt Leviant. A novel by one of the finest living Yiddish poets and prose writers. Set in Vilna between the World Wars, the story focuses on a woman whose husband is lost in war but not officially dead. Bobbs-Merrill, 1975, $6.95.

GREEN, GERALD. *The Last Angry Man.* One of the finest novels about Jewish life in America, the drive for achievement, the thirst for social justice. Pocket Books, 1972, $1.25.

GROSS, THEODORE. *The Literature of American Jews.* A collection of short segments of popular, important American-Jewish novels. Macmillan, 1973, $12.95.

HAZAZ, HAIM. *Gates of Bronze.* A panoramic vision of the shtetl's disintegration in the maelstrom of the Russian Revolution. Jewish Publication Society, 1975, $7.95.

HOWE, IRVING, and GREENBERG, ELIEZER. *A Treasury of Yiddish Poetry.* An anthology of poems of the shtetl, of Jewish intimacy with God, of revolutionaries and immigrants, and of voices from the Holocaust. Schocken, 1976, $5.95 paperback.

—————————. *A Treasury of Yiddish Stories.* An anthology of classic and modern tales. Schocken Books, 1973, $5.50 paperback.

KOSSOFF, DAVID. *The Voices of Massada.* A fictionalized account of the zealots in their desert stronghold, by an English-Jewish actor. St. Martin's Press, 1973, $6.95.

LANDIS, JOSEPH C. *The Great Jewish Plays.* Full texts of six classic Yiddish plays, including *The Golem, The Dybbuk, The God of Vengeance,* in new translation. Horizon, 1972, $7.95. Avon-Equinox, $3.95 paperback.

LEVIN, MEYER. *The Old Bunch.* Novel about a group of Jewish youngsters who grew up in Chicago. Macfadden, 1937, $.95.

—————————. *The Settlers.* Massive family chronicle beginning in

Palestine at the turn of the century and continuing to the modern period. Set against the history of the Yishuv with recognizable portraits of its leaders. Simon and Schuster, 1972, $9.95; Pocket Books, $1.75 paperback.

MALAMUD, BERNARD. *The Assistant.* The story of the struggles of a neighborhood grocer, his daughter, and the non-Jew who falls in love with her. Dell, 1971, $1.25 paperback.

—————————. *The Fixer.* Novel based on the infamous Beiliss blood accusation trial. Pocket Books, 1975, $2.25 paperback.

—————————. *Idiots First.* A collection of short stories. Farrar, Straus and Giroux, 1963, $6.95; Pocket Books, 1976, $1.75 paperback.

—————————. *The Magic Barrel.* A collection of compassionate and perceptive short stories. Farrar, Straus and Giroux, 1958, $5.95; Pocket Books, 1976, $1.25 paperback.

MICHENER, JAMES, ed. *Firstfruits: A Harvest of 25 Years of Israeli Writing.* Fifteen short stories from leading Israeli authors. Jewish Publication Society, 1973, $6.95; Fawcett, 1974, $1.75 paperback.

—————————. *The Source.* An encounter with Jewish history through the site of an archaeological dig. Fawcett, $2.50 paperback.

NISSENSON, HUGH. *A Pile of Stones: In the Reign of Peace.* Eight short stories of situations and people in Israel. Farrar, Straus & Giroux, 1972, $5.95; Curtis, 1973, $.95 paperback.

OZ, AMOS. *Elsewhere Perhaps.* Of human relationships on a kibbutz in the 1960's. Harcourt Brace Jovanovich, 1973, $7.95; Bantam, 1974, $1.50 paperback.

—————————. *My Michael.* A best seller in Israel. In this novel about the middle class in Jerusalem, Mr. Oz deals with not only wars and uncertainties in Israel, but also with relationships between men and women, Arabs and Jews. Knopf, 1972, $6.95; Bantam, 1975, $1.95 paperback.

OZICK, CYNTHIA. *The Pagan Rabbi and Other Stories.* Two novellas and four short stories. Knopf, 1971, $6.95; Schocken, 1976, $3.45 paperback.

PERETZ, I. L. *Selected Stories.* Edited with an introduction by Irving Howe and Eliezer Greenberg. Schocken, 1975, $6.95; $2.95 paperback.

POTOK, CHAIM. *My Name is Asher Lev.* A novel depicting the conflict between the religious and secular worlds through the development of a young Jewish artist. Fawcett, 1972, $1.75 paperback.

—————————. *The Chosen.* The story of an Orthodox boy and his friend, son of a Hassidic rebbe. Fawcett, 1968, $1.50 paperback.

—————————. *The Promise.* Sequel to *The Chosen,* this novel continues the story of Reuven and Danny, who have now become a rabbi and a clinical psychologist, respectively. Knopf, 1969, $6.95; Fawcett, 1973, $1.50 paperback.

—————————. *In the Beginning.* The author takes us back to the thirties and forties, to show us the turbulent education of a scholar, in a novel of Jewish family life. Knopf, 1975, $8.95; Fawcett, 1976, $1.95 paperback.

ROTH, HENRY. *Call It Sleep.* An early (1934) important novel of American Jewish life. Avon, 1964, $1.75 paperback.

ROTH, PHILIP. *Goodbye, Columbus.* A novella and collection of short stories dealing with Jewish life in America. Bantam Books, 1970, $1.25 paperback.

SAMUEL, MAURICE. *The Second Crucifixion.* A novel set in 2nd century Rome about the seeds of anti-Semitism. It tells about the clash between the Ebionites, a tiny sect of Jews who accepted Jesus as teacher and prophet, and the early Church Fathers. Knopf, 1960, $4.95.

SHAHAR, DAVID. *News from Jerusalem.* Fifteen short stories by a prize-winning Israeli author, winner of the 1973 Agnon Prize. Houghton Mifflin, 1974, $6.95.

FICTION AND DRAMA

SINGER, ISAAC BASHEVIS. *A Crown of Feathers.* Twenty-four short stories set in the United States and Europe, among other places. Farrar, Straus & Giroux, 1973, $7.95; Fawcett, 1974, $1.50 paperback.

——————. *The Family Moskat.* Chronicle spanning the life of a Jewish family in Warsaw from the mid-nineteenth century to the end of World War II. Fawcett, 1975, $1.95 paperback.

——————. *Gimpel the Fool and Other Stories.* Set against the ghetto world of 19th century Poland. Avon, 1964, $.75. Out of print. Other titles: *The Slave,* Avon, 1971, $1.25; *Enemies, A Love Story,* Fawcett, 1973, $1.25; *Spinoza of Market Street,* Avon, 1966, $1.95.

SINGER, I. J. *Brothers Ashkenazi.* Saga of the city of Lodz. Knopf, 1936, $5.95; World Publishing, $3.45 paperback.

STEINBERG, MILTON. *As a Driven Leaf.* A fictional biography of Elisha ben Abuyah in Hellenistic Palestine of the second century. Behrman House, 1939, $4.95 paperback.

WALDEN, DANIEL, ed. *On Being Jewish: American-Jewish Writers from Cahan to Bellow.* Fawcett, 1975, $1.75 paperback.

WALLANT, EDWARD LEWIS. *The Pawnbroker.* A former teacher in Poland whose family was liquidated by the Nazis tries to find new meaning in his life as a pawnbroker in Harlem. Manor Books, 1962, 1975, $1.50.

WIESEL, ELIE. *A Beggar in Jerusalem.* Avon, 1970, $1.25.

——————. *Gates of the Forest.* Gregor, a young Hungarian Jew who escapes the Nazis, must face the contemporary crisis of the soul. Holt, Rinehart and Winston, 1966, $4.95; Avon, 1969, $1.75 paperback.

——————. *Legends of Our Time.* Brilliant, memorable narratives, part fantasy, part fact. Holt, Rinehart and Winston, 1968, $5.95; Avon, 1970, $1.25 paperback.

————. *The Oath.* A man's loyalty to the dead may become another's reason to go on living. Random, 1973, $7.95; Avon, $1.75 paperback.

————. *Zalman or the Madness of God.* A play about Soviet Jewry. Random, 1975, $6.95. (See *Russian Jews,* also *Holocaust.*)

WISSE, RUTH, ed. and trans. *A Shtetl and Other Yiddish Novellas.* Works written from 1900 to 1915 by Bergelson, Opatoshu, Ansky, Weissenberg, and Mendele. Behrman House, 1973, $12.50.

YUDKIN, LEON ISRAEL. *Escape into Siege.* A survey of modern Israeli literature. Routeledge and Kegan Paul, 1974, $11.75.

GENERAL

ADLER, MORRIS, ed. *The Jewish Heritage Reader*. A wealth of articles on a variety of Jewish subjects from the *Jewish Heritage Magazine*. B'nai Brith/Taplinger, 1965, $5.95 paperback.

BELLIN, MILDRED. *The Jewish Cook Book*. Bloch, 1958, $5.95.

GOLDIN, JUDAH. *On a Selective Bibliography in English for the Study of Judaism in Charles J. Adams' (ed.) "A Reader's Guide to the Great Religions."* A bibliographical essay for the serious student covering general works on Judaism and Jewish History and specific works on the Biblical, Hellenistic, Rabbinic and Gaonic periods. The essay itself reveals much about these subjects. Free Press, 1965, $10.95.

GOODMAN, HANNA. *Jewish Cooking Around the World*. Favorite recipes of Jewish communities around the world. Recipes are arranged according to holidays and also geographically. Illustrated. Jewish Publication Society, 1965, $6.95.

GREENBERG, SIDNEY. *A Treasury of the Art of Living*. A useful collection of readings. Wilshire Press, 1964, $2.00 paperback.

————. *A Treasury of Comfort*. Readings relating to death and mourning. Borden, 1967, $2.50 paperback.

GROSSINGER, JENNIE. *The Art of Jewish Cooking*. Bantam Books, 1969, $1.25 paperback.

KUSHNER, LAWRENCE. *The Book of Letters: A Mystical Alef-Bait*. Meanings and ideas found in the twenty-two letters of the Hebrew alphabet captured in this calligraphic work. Harper & Row, 1975, $6.95.

POSNER, RAPHAEL, general editor. *Popular Judaica Library*. These small-sized, illustrated books include the following titles: Marriage, Family, High Holy Days, The Synagogue, Minor and Major Festivals, The Return to Zion, Hassidism. Amiel, $3.95 each, cloth.

SIEGEL, RICHARD, and STRASSFIELD, MICHAEL and SUSAN, eds. *The Jewish Catalog*. A compendium of practical information on a wide

wide variety of topics, designed for personal creative expression of the Jewish experience. Jewish Publication Society, 1973, $5.95 paperback. Volume 2 expected Fall, 1976.

——————. *Jewish Calendar.* A calendar for desk or large pockets chock full of Jewish information and information about Jews, published annually. Universe Books, 1976, $3.95.

TRACHTENBERG, JOSHUA. *Jewish Magic and Superstition.* Atheneum, 1970, $4.95.

HASIDISM

BEN-AMOS, DAN, and MINTZ, JEROME R., eds. *In Praise of the Baal Shem Tov.* The earliest collection of legends about the founder of Hasidism. A translation of "Shivche HaBesht" by Rabbi Jacob Joseph of Polnoye. Indiana University Press, 1972, $3.95 paperback.

BEN ZION, RAPHAEL, ed. *An Anthology of Jewish Mysticism.* Contains Cordovero's "Palm Tree of Deborah," Schneur Zalman's "Portal of Unity and Faith," and R. Hayim Volozhin's "Nefesh HaChayim." Yesod Publishers, 1945, $5.00.

BOKSER, BEN ZION. *From the World of the Cabbalah, A Portrait of Rabbi Judah Loew, the Maharal of Prague.* (16th century.) Philosophical Library, 1954, $3.00.

BUBER, MARTIN. *For the Sake of Heaven.* Ludwig Lewisohn, trans. Atheneum, 1953, $3.45 paperback.

——————. *Hasidism and Modern Man.* Translated by Maurice Friedman. A series of essays distilling the core of Hasidic teaching: that "man cannot approach the divine by reaching beyond the human; he can approach Him through becoming human." To become human is what he has been created for. Harper & Row, 1966, $2.50 paperback.

——————. *Origin and Meaning of Hasidism.* Buber's recreation and interpretation of Hasidism, less concerned with defining theoretical concepts than with pointing to an image of man, a way of life. Horizon Press, 1972, $3.45 paperback.

——————. *Tales of the Hasidim.* Originally the recitals by disciples of the miraculous deeds and profound sayings of the Zaddikim, they were passed on from generation to generation for two centuries. Schocken Books, 1947, 2 vols., $3.25 and $3.45 paperback.

——————. *The Tales of Rabbi Nachman.* A selection of the tales and sayings of this great Hasidic master, with a short essay on Jewish mysticism. Avon, 1970, $1.45 paperback.

—————————. *Ten Rungs: Hasidic Sayings.* Homilies probing the inner dynamics of man's spiritual growth. Schocken, 1962, $1.75 paperback.

DRESNER, SAMUEL H. *Levi Yitzhak of Berdichev.* A portrait of a Hasidic master, one of the outstanding personalities in the history of religion. Hartmore House, 1974, $10.00.

—————————. *The Zaddik.* The doctrine of the zaddik, according to the writings of Rabbi Jacob Yosef of Polnoye, one of the direct disciples of the Baal Shem Tov. Schocken, 1974, $3.45 paperback.

HEINERMAN, BEN, ed. *The Maggid of Dubnow and His Parables.* Philip Feldheim, 1967. Out of print.

JACOBS, LOUIS. *Hasidic Prayer.* Highly recommended motivating key to a spiritual world. Schocken, 1973, $10.00.

KAPLAN, ARYEH, and ROSENFELD, ZVI A. *Rabbi Nachman's Wisdom.* "Shivche HaRan" and "Sichos HaRan"—teachings ranging from everyday advice to sublime Kabbalistic mysteries, as recorded by his disciple, R. Nathan of Nemirov. Sepher Hermon Press, 1975, $8.95.

LEVIN, MEYER. *Hasidic Tales.* Tales of the life and wondrous deeds of the Baal Shem Tov and Rabbi Nachman of Bratzlav. Penguin Books, 1975, $3.95.

LIVNEH, ELIEZER. "Judaism and the Religions of the Far East." *Judaism,* Vol. 6, No. 3 (Summer, 1957). A comparison of the dominant themes of two types of religion, emphasizing the important differences between them.

MINTZ, JEROME R. *Legends of the Hasidim.* An introduction to Hasidic culture and oral tradition in the New World. University of Chicago Press, 1968, $5.95 paperback.

NEWMAN, LOUIS. *The Hasidic Anthology: Tales and Teachings of the Hasidim.*

Schocken Books, 1963, $5.95 paperback.

—————————. *Maggidim and Hasidim: Their Wisdom.* Bloch, 1962, $5.50.

PONCE, CHARLES. *Kabbalah: An Introduction and Illumination for the World Today.* A modern treatment which not only surveys the traditional aspects of Jewish mysticism and Kabbalah, but includes psychological aspects and Eastern mysticism. Straight Arrow Books, 1973, $5.95 paperback.

RABINOWITZ, HARRY. *The World of Hasidism.* A presentation of history and personalities. Hartmore House, 1970, $6.95.

ROSKIES, DIANE and DAVID G. *The Shtetl Book.* In-depth study of one shtetl in Eastern Europe plus an overview of the major patterns and events shaping the life of Eastern European Jewry. Ktav, 1975, $10.00 cloth; $5.95 paperback.

SCHACHTER, ZALMAN. *Fragments of a Future Scroll: Hasidism for the Aquarian Age.* Hasidism, mysticism and Kabbalah—translations from relevant source materials. Leaves of Grass Press, 1975, $3.95 paperback.

SCHOLEM, GERSHOM. *Kabbalah.* The most up-to-date survey of Jewish mysticism. Quadrangle/N.Y. Times Book Co., 1974, $15.00.

—————————. *Major Trends in Jewish Mysticism.* A survey and re-thinking of the role of mysticism in Jewish history. Schocken, 1961, $3.95 paperback.

—————————. *On the Kabbalah and Its Symbolism.* A collection of essays. Schocken, 1965, $2.25.

—————————. *The Messianic Idea in Judaism: And Other Essays on Jewish Spirituality.* Description of a powerful force within Jewish history. Schocken, 1972, $3.95.

—————————. *Shabbatai Sevi: The Mystical Prince and Messiah.* The false messiah and his era. Princeton, 1973, $25.00 cloth; 1975, $9.50 paperback.

—————————, ed. *The Zohar: The Book of Splendor.* Brief, representative selections from the chief work of Kabbalah literature. Schocken, 1949, $1.75 paperback.

SIMON, MAURICE, and SPERLING, HARRY, translators. *The Zohar.* The fundamental work of the Spanish Kabbalah, taking the form of a commentary on the Torah. Soncino Press, 1934, five volumes, $75.00; Rebecca Bennet Edition, reprint, $40.00.

WEINER, HERBERT. *9½ Mystics. The Kabbala Today.* A treasure hunt for the life secrets of the mystical tradition as it exists today. Collier Books, 1971, $1.95 paperback.

WENGROW, CHARLES. *Baal Shem Tov on Pirke Avot.* (Translated and edited.) Homiletic commentary on "Ethics of the Fathers" by the founder of Hasidism. Philip Feldheim, 1974, $7.50.

WIESEL, ELIE. *Souls on Fire.* Portraits and stories of the leaders of the Hasidic movements: The Baal Shem Tov, Rabbi Nachman, Israel of Ryszyn, and the Kotzker Rebbe. Handy chronological table of world events provides interesting backdrop. Random House, 1972, $6.95 cloth; $1.65 paperback.

ZALMAN, SCHNEUR (of Liadi). *Tanya (Likutei Amarim).* The classic work expounding basic Chassidic principles by the founder of Chabad-Chassidism. Introduction, notes, English text. Kehot, 1968-72, 5 volumes, $1.50-$5.50.

HISTORY: GENERAL AND SOCIOLOGY

AGUS, JACOB B. *The Meaning of Jewish History.* Two volumes, Abelard-Schuman, 1963, $10.50.

BARON, SALO W., and KAHN, ARCADIUS, et al. *Economic History of the Jews.* A general survey, followed by sections on Jewish activities in specific branches of the economy. Schocken Books, 1975, $15.00.

—————————. *The Jewish Community.* A sociological history of the Jewish community throughout the ages. Three volumes. Greenwood Press, 1972, $42.50.

—————————. *Modern Nationalism and Religion.* History and analysis of various nationalistic movements and religions and their antagonism. Books for Librarians, 1947, $13.00.

—————————. *A Social and Religious History of the Jews.* The definitive contemporary work on Jewish social, political, economic, and cultural history, with emphasis on motifs rather than strict chronology. Extensive notes provide an exhaustive bibliography. Fifteen volumes published thus far, from the Biblical period to the 17th century. Jewish Publication Society and Columbia Univ., 1952-1973, $12.50 per volume.

BEN-SASSON, H. H., and ETTINGER, S. *Jewish Society Throughout the Ages.* A collection of essays from the faculties of the Hebrew University of Jerusalem. Schocken Books, 1969, $3.95 paperback.

DIMONT, MAX. *Jews, God and History* and *The Indestructible Jews.* Two volumes that make a case for Jewish manifest destiny. NAL Mentor 1972, 1973, $1.50 each paperback.

DUBNOW, SIMON. *History of the Jews.* (See listing under *Reference.*)

ECKMAN, LESTER. *The History of the Musar Movement, 1840-1945.* A brief summary. Shengold Publishers, 1975, $8.95.

FINKELSTEIN, LOUIS, ed. *The Jews.* Three volumes of essays spanning the total range of history, culture and thought. Schocken Books,

Vol. I—History, 1970, $4.95; Vol. II—Religion and Culture, 1971, $4.50; Vol. III—Role in Civilization, 1971, $5.95.

FRIED, JACOB, ed. *Judaism and the Community.* A collection of articles dealing with the social problems that confront the Jew in the 20th century. A. S. Barnes, $6.00.

GRAETZ, HEINRICH. *History of the Jews.* English translation of the classic work by the great Jewish historian; chronological tables of the modern era. Jewish Publication Society, 1898, 6 volumes, $30.00.

GRAYZEL, SOLOMON. *History of the Jews.* A popular one-volume history of the Jews from the Babylonian Exile to the present day. 125 illustrations and 24 maps. Jewish Publication Society, 1968, $6.00; NAL, 1975, $1.95 paperback.

HENKIN, LOUIS. *World Politics and the Jewish Condition.* A collection of essays by eminent political authorities, assessing developments in the Jewish world of the seventies. Quadrangle, 1972, $9.95.

KATZMAN, JACOB. *Jewish Influence on Civilization.* The important Jewish contributions to human endeavor since Bible times. Bloch, 1974, $7.95.

LESLAU, WOLF. *Falasha Anthology: The Black Jews of Ethiopia.* Their history and social organization and an anthology of their sacred writings. Schocken Books, 1969, $2.45. Out of print.

LEVY, ISAAC. *The Synagogue: Its History and Function.* Biblical and Rabbinic literature, archaeology, organization and growth, structure and equipment, personnel, modes of worship and their sources. Vallentine Mitchell (Hartmore House), 1963, $3.95 cloth.

LIEBERMAN, SAUL, and HYMAN, ARTHUR, eds. *Salo Wittmayer Baron Jubilee Volume.* A Festschrift in three volumes, dedicated to the eminent historian and teacher on the occasion of his 80th birthday. Columbia University Press, 1975, $60.00.

MARGOLIS, MAX, and MARX, ALEXANDER. *A History of the Jewish People.* A single-volume history. Atheneum, 1969, $5.95 paperback.

MARTIN, BERNARD, and SILVER, DANIEL JEREMY. *History of Judaism.* Two volumes of lively writing. Basic Books, 1975, $37.00.

MAZAR, BENJAMIN, and DAVIS, MOSHE. *The Illustrated History of the Jews.* Pictorial, historical survey. Israel, Publishing Institute, 1963, $30.00. (Illustrated World of the Bible Library—B. Mazar & Michael Avi-Yonah, 4 volumes, Davey, 1961, $80.00.)

MEYER, MICHAEL A., ed. *Ideas of Jewish History.* Despite the vicissitudes of their historical experience, the Jews survive as an identifiable entity. Behrman House, 1974, $12.50; 1975, $4.95 paperback.

ROTH, CECIL. *A History of the Jews from Earliest Times Through the Six-Day War.* Schocken Books, 1970, $3.95 paperback.

SACHAR, ABRAM. *History of the Jews.* Alfred A. Knopf, 1964, $5.25 paperback.

SCHWARTZ, LEO W., ed. *Great Ages and Ideas of the Jewish People.* Essays by eminent scholars on selected periods of Jewish History. Modern Library, 1962, $5.95. Out of print.

TREPP, LEO. *A History of the Jewish Experience: Eternal Faith, Eternal People.* A well-rounded presentation that emphasizes history, thought, and observance. Behrman House, 1973, $4.95.

HISTORY: ANCIENT AND ARCHAEOLOGY

BRIGHT, JOHN. *A History of Israel.* History of the Jewish people from its beginnings to the Maccabean revolt. Maps and chronological tables and a discussion of Near Eastern history and culture before the appearance of the Hebrews. Westminster, 1972, $10.95.

CERAM, C. W. *The Secret of the Hittites: The Discovery of an Ancient Empire.* The archaeological discovery of the ancient empire which may have extended across the Biblical Israel of Abraham's time. Schocken Books, 1973, $3.95.

DUCKAT, WALTER. *Beggar to King: All Occupations of Biblical Times.* What they did and how they did it. A survey of more than 200 trades and callings. Doubleday, $5.95; Abingdon, 1971, $2.95 paperback.

EHRLICH, ERNEST LUDWIG. *A Concise History of Israel: From the Earliest Times to the Destruction of the Temple in 70 A.D.* Translated by James Barr. Harper & Row, 1962, $1.75 paperback.

FINEGAN, JACK. *Light From the Ancient Past.* Archaeological background of the Judaeo-Christian religions. (Volume II covers the New Testament period.) Princeton Univ. Press, 1969, $3.95 each.

FRANKFORT, HENRI, et al. *Before Philosophy: The Intellectual Adventure of Ancient Man.* Four essays on the nature of myth and mythopoeic thinking characterizing the religions of the ancient Near East, and the radical departures represented by Biblical religion and Greek philosophy. Provides the essential background for the intellectual and religious history of Western civilization. Penguin Books, 1949, $1.75 paperback.

—————————. *Birth of Civilization in the Near East.* Detailed but clear study of ancient Mesopotamia and Egypt. Anchor, 1959, $1.95 paperback.

GASTER, THEODORE H. *The Dead Sea Scriptures.* A translation of the Scrolls with introduction and notes by Dr. Gaster. Doubleday-Anchor, 1956, $2.50 paperback.

GRAY, JOHN. *Archaeology and the Old Testament World.* An introduction to the mind of ancient Israel in her historical and cultural environment. Gannon, 1962, $7.50.

HALLO, WILLIAM W., and SIMPSON, WILLIAM K. *The Ancient Near East: A History.* Harcourt Brace Jovanovich, 1972, $5.50 paperback.

KRAMER, SAMUEL N. *The Sumerians: Their History, Culture and Character.* University of Chicago Press, 1971, $2.95 paperback.

——————————. *Sumerian Mythology.* An authoritative sketch of the mythological patterns of the ancient world underlying much of Biblical literature. Univ. of Pennsylvania Press, 1972, $2.95 paperback.

LANDAY, JERRY M. *Silent Cities, Sacred Stones: Archaeological Discovery in Israel.* An exciting, grandly illustrated account of the major archaeological finds in Israel. Saturday Review Press, 1971, $14.95.

NEGEV, AVRAHAM, ed. *Archaeological Encyclopedia of the Holy Land.* Putnam, 1972, $15.95.

OESTERLY, W. O. *History of Israel.* Oxford University Press, 1932, 2 volumes, $4.75 each.

OPPENHEIM, A. LEO. *Ancient Mesopotamia: Portrait of a Dead Civilization.* University of Chicago Press, 1964, $3.95.

ORLINSKY, HARRY. *Ancient Israel.* A brief survey. Cornell University Press, 1960, $1.95 paperback.

PAUL, SHOLOM M., and DEVER, WILLIAM G. *Biblical Archaeology.* A fascinating record of the past. Harper & Row, 1973, $12.50.

PRITCHARD, JAMES, ed. *Ancient Near Eastern Texts.* Paperback reprint of the famous and continually cited "A.N.E.T." A collection of epigraphical discoveries with ample footnotes and cross references to parallel passages in Biblical literature. Princeton University Press, 1969, $30 cloth; 1973, $3.95 paperback (Vol. I).

———————. *Archaeology and the Old Testament.* Archaeology has supplemented knowledge of Biblical persons and places during the last one hundred years. Princeton University Press, 1958, $2.95 paperback.

YADIN, YIGAEL. *Hazor: The Rediscovery of a Great Citadel of the Bible.* An exciting detective story, uncovering 22 cities dating to 2500 B.C.E. Random House, 1975, $20.00.

HISTORY: HELLENISTIC & RABBINIC PERIODS

AVI-YONAH, MICHAEL, and BARAS, ZVI. *The Herodian Period.* A collection of studies by outstanding scholars. A volume in the World History of the Jewish People. Rutgers University Press, 1975, $25.00.

BICKERMAN, ELIAS. *From Ezra to the Last of the Maccabees: Foundations of Post-Biblical Judaism.* The influence of Hellenistic culture on post-exile Judaism. Schocken Books, 1962, $1.95 paperback.

COMAY, JOAN. *The Temple of Jerusalem.* A history of the Temple from earliest times, based upon Biblical and archaeological records. Lavishly illustrated. Holt, Rinehart and Winston, 1975, $15.00.

GRANT, MICHAEL. *The Jews in the Roman World.* Scribner's, 1973, $10.00.

HADAS, MOSES. *Hellenistic Culture: Fusion and Diffusion.* It was in the Hellenistic age, after the conquests of Alexander the Great, that disparate cultural traditions interacted upon one another to fix the permanent contours of European civilization. Norton, 1959, $2.65 paperback.

HENGEL, MARTIN. *Judaism and Hellenism.* An inter-testamental study of the cultural encounter in Palestine during the early Hellenistic period. Fortress Press, 1975, $34.00 set.

JOSEPHUS, FLAVIUS. *Complete Works.* Holt, Rinehart and Winston, 1957, $15.95.

——————————. *The Jewish War.* Archaeological finds continue to reveal the accuracy of these classic first century accounts of Jewish life. Penguin, 1959, $1.95 paperback.

——————————. *The Second Jewish Commonwealth.* A history extending from the Maccabean War to the outbreak of the Roman war, 66 CE. Schocken, 1971, $4.50 paperback.

MAZAR, BENJAMIN. *The Mountain of the Lord.* The study of the vital new archaeological discoveries at Jerusalem's Temple Mount, in search for Herod's Temple. Lavishly illustrated. Doubleday, 1975, $30.00.

HISTORY: HELLENISTIC AND RABBINIC PERIODS

NEUSNER, JACOB. *There We Sat Down: Talmudic Judaism in the Making.* The character of Judaism in the age that shaped the classical tradition. Abingdon Press, 1972, $2.95.

——————. *First Century Judaism in Crisis.* A biography of R. Yohanan ben Zakkai who, after the destruction of the Temple, set the future course for Judaism. Abingdon Press, 1975, $4.50 paperback.

PEARLMAN, MOSHE. *The Maccabees.* History of the Maccabean War and the Hasmonean kings. Photographs. Macmillan, 1973, $12.95.

PETERS, F. E. *The Harvest of Hellenism.* Various aspects of Hellenistic life over a vast area. Includes the Seleucid/Ptolemaic struggle over Judea. The Roman conquest and matters Jewish are treated in passing. Simon & Schuster, 1971, $4.95.

RABIN, CHAIM. *Qumran Studies.* Detailed essays demonstrating the connection and continuity between Pharasaic Judaism and the Dead Sea Scrolls. Schocken Books, 1975, $3.95 paperback.

RADIN, MAX. *The Jews Among the Greeks and Romans.* Arno, reprint of 1915 edition, $23.00.

SCHOENFIELD, HUGH J. *The Jesus Party.* Pursuing the theory in his previous work, *The Passover Plot,* the author traces the history of the loyal followers of Jesus after his death. Macmillan, 1975, $7.95.

SCHURER, EMIL. *A History of the Jewish People in the Time of Jesus.* A detailed survey of the major issues of the early Rabbinic period. Schocken Books, 1961, $2.45 paperback.

——————. *The Literature of the Jewish People in the Time of Jesus.* Schocken Books, 1972, $4.50 paperback.

SHALIT, ABRAHAM, ed. *The Hellenistic Age.* Collection of outstanding essays. A volume in the World History of the Jewish People. Rutgers Univ. Press, $20.00.

SIMON, MARCEL. *Jewish Sects in the Time of Jesus.* A brilliant, short essay giving a perspective for each of many fascinating sects. Translated by J. H. Forley. Fortress Press, 1967, $3.50 paperback.

TCHERIKOVER, VICTOR. *Hellenistic Civilization and the Jews.* An indispensable survey of Jewish history from Alexander until the last of the Maccabees. Atheneum, 1970, $4.75 paperback.

YADIN, YIGAEL. *Bar-Kokhba.* A record of the discoveries in the Judean Desert of 1960-61; rich in color photographs. Random House, 1971, $15.00.

——————. *Message of the Scrolls.* Simon & Schuster, 1967, $5.95; 1969, $1.45 paperback.

——————. *Masada: Herod's Fortress and the Zealots Last Stand.* An illustrated account of Masada by the archaeologist who unearthed it. Random House, 1966, $15.00.

ZEITLIN, SOLOMON. *The Rise and Fall of the Judean State.* A political, social, and religious history of the Second Commonwealth. Vol. I— 332-37 BCE; Vol. II—37 BCE-66 CE. Jewish Publication Society, 1967, $15.00, two volumes.

HISTORY: MEDIEVAL AND RENAISSANCE

ABRAHAMS, ISRAEL. *Jewish Life in the Middle Ages.* A pleasant narrative account of Jewish life in the towns of medieval Ashkenaz. Atheneum, 1969, $4.25 paperback.

ADLER, ELKAN N. *Jewish Travelers.* Interesting, often overlooked members of the medieval Jewish world. Hermon Press, 1930, $5.75.

ANKORI, ZVI. *Karaites in Byzantium: The Formative Years, 970-1100.* AMS Press, 1959, $15.00.

BAER, YITZHAK. *Galut.* The application of Zionist historiography to the Jew's life and situation in medieval Ashkenaz. Schocken Books, 1947, $1.50 paperback.

——————. *A History of the Jews in Christian Spain.* The Jewish experience in the Iberian Peninsula from the earliest dispersions until the final expulsion in 1492. Jewish Publication Society, 1966, 2 vols., $12.00 set.

BARON, SALO W. *Essays on Ancient and Medieval Jewish History.* These essays maintain a positive view of Galut and feature copious footnotes. Rutgers Univ. Press, 1973, $12.50.

BEN-ZVI, YITZHAK. *The Exiled and the Redeemed.* An interesting description of some exotic medieval Jewish communities. Jewish Publication Society, 1961, $4.50.

COHEN, GERSON D., trans. *Sefer HaQubbuluh: The Book of Tradition, by Abraham ibn Daud.* The introductory essay offers a series of insights into the mind of the medieval Jewish community. Jewish Publication Society, 1967 $7.50.

GOITEIN, SOLOMON D. *Jews and Arabs, Their Contacts Through the Ages.* The most easily read treatment of medieval Jewish life under Islam. Schocken Books, $3.45 paperback. Revised and updated, 1974.

KATZ, JACOB. *Tradition and Crisis.* An important study of the Jewish community on the eve of Emancipation. Schocken Books, 1971, $2.95 paperback.

HISTORY: MEDIEVAL AND RENAISSANCE

MARCUS, JACOB R. *The Jew in the Medieval World.* An annotated collection of documents. Atheneum, reprint of 1938 edition, 1969, $5.95 paperback.

NEMOY, LEON. *Karaite Anthology.* Key works and thinkers of Karaism. Yale Univ. Press, 1952, $12.50.

ROTH, CECIL, ed. *The Dark Ages.* Jews in Christian Europe, 700-1096. An important collection of essays. Part of the World History of the Jewish People. Rutgers Univ. Press, 1966, $20.00.

——————. *A History of the Marranos.* Schocken Books, 1975, $5.50 paperback.

——————. *Jews in the Renaissance.* Peter Smith, 1959, $5.00; Harper, 1965, $2.45 paperback.

——————. *History of the Jews in Venice.* Social history of a Jewish community that became an important meeting place between Jews of the East and West during the 16th and 17th centuries. Schocken Books, 1975, $6.50 paperback.

SHARF, ANDREW. *Byzantine Jewry: From Justinian to the Fourth Crusade.* A short summary of the lifespan of the Jewish communities in Byzantium. Schocken Books, 1971, $7.50.

STERN, SELMA. *The Court Jew.* A history of this special institution and the colorful but often dangerous careers of these Jewish spokesmen. Jewish Publication Society, 1950, out of print.

YERUSHALMI, YOSEF HAYIM. *From Spanish Court to Italian Ghetto.* A well-written, absorbing re-analysis of Maranno life. Columbia Univ. Press, 1971, $20.00.

CHAZAN, ROBERT, and RAPHAEL, MARC LEE, eds. *Modern Jewish History: A Source Reader*. Significant developments and trends in Jewish history from the French Revolution to the present, in excerpts from the works of leading Jewish scholars, writers, philosophers and political leaders. Schocken Books, 1975, $7.95 paperback.

DAWIDOWICZ, LUCY. *The Golden Tradition: Jewish Life and Thought in Eastern Europe*. Documents and autobiographical materials on the history of Eastern European Jewry. Holt, Rinehart and Winston, 1967, $8.95. Beacon, $3.95 paperback.

DUBNOW, SIMON. *History of the Jews in Russia and Poland*. History of these communities from their medieval origins until World War I. Ktav, rev. ed., 1973, $25.00.

————————. *Nationalism and History*. A collection of essays dealing primarily with the modern era. Atheneum, 1970, $4.50 paperback.

GLAZER, NATHAN, and MOYNIHAN, DANIEL P. *Ethnicity: Theory and Experience*. Ethnicity has played a pivotal role in recent social changes as an effective means for advancing group interests. Harvard Univ. Press, 1975, $15.00.

GORDIS, ROBERT. *The Root and the Branch: Judaism and the Free Society*. The insights and values of the Jewish tradition brought to the problems of democracy, racial tension, religious liberty, the relationship of church and state, and international relations. University of Chicago, 1962, $9.00.

HERTZBERG, ARTHUR. *The French Enlightenment and the Jews*. The origins of modern anti-Semitism. A history of the Jews of Enlightenment France, and a re-evaluation of the relationship of this era to the rise of modern anti-Semitism. Schocken Books, 1970, $3.95 paperback.

KATZ, JACOB. *Out of the Ghetto: The Social Background of Jewish Emancipation: 1770-1870*. The latest contribution of this fine scholar to the analysis of the Emancipation era. Harvard Univ. Press, 1973, $12.00.

————————. *Exclusiveness and Tolerance. On Jewish-Gentile Relations in Medieval and Modern Times*. Schocken Books, 1962, $3.45 paperback.

LIPTZIN, SOLOMON C. *Germany's Stepchildren.* Biographies of famous Jewish-German personalities from the Enlightenment to the Nazi era investigate the tragic duality in the Jewish soul vis-a-vis the majority culture. Books for Libraries, reprint of the 1944 edition, $14.50.

MAHLER, RAPHAEL. *The History of Modern Jewry: 1780-1815.* The best one-volume statement; heavily documented. Schocken Books, 1971, $15.00.

MEYER, MICHAEL A. *The Origins of the Modern Jew: Jewish Identity and European Culture in Germany, 1749-1824.* Fine treatment of the period. Wayne State Univ. Press, 1972, $3.95.

PHILIPSON, DAVID. *The Reform Movement in Judaism.* The classic statement by one of the early leaders of the Movement. Ktav, 1931, $15.00.

PLAUT, W. GUNTHER. *The Rise of Reform Judaism: A Sourcebook of Its European Origins. The Growth of Reform Judaism: American and European Sources.* A record of the significant developments in the history of the Reform Movement in the words of its leading exponents. U.A.H.C., 1963, 1965, $7.50 each volume.

SACHAR, HOWARD M. *The Course of Modern Jewish History.* From the Enlightenment to the establishment of the State of Israel. Dell, 1958, $4.45 paperback.

SHIRER, WILLIAM L. *The Rise and Fall of the Third Reich.* (See listing under *Holocaust.*)

WEINRYB, BERNARD. *The Jews of Poland: A Social and Economic History of the Jewish Community in Poland.* A thorough history from 1100 to 1800 by a leading scholar. 1974 Jewish Book Council History Award. Jewish Publication Society, 1973, $10.00.

ZBOROWSKI, MARK, and HERZOG, ELIZABETH. *Life Is With People: The Culture of the Shtetl.* A sociological discussion of Jewish life in the small towns of Eastern Europe. Schocken Books, 1962, $3.95 paperback.

HOLOCAUST

ARENDT, HANNAH. *Eichmann in Jerusalem.* Viking, 1963, $1.95.

—————————. *The Origins of Totalitarianism.* Massive, controversial study of these modern political systems. Harcourt Brace Jovanovich, 1973, $4.95 paperback.

AVRIEL, EHUD. *Open the Gates.* The rescue of European Jews by Mossad, and their subsequent entry into Palestine. Atheneum, 1974, $10.00.

BARKAI, MEYER. *The Fighting Ghettos.* An anthology of eye-witness reports and memoirs of resistance and partisan fighting against the Nazis in the ghettos, forests, and concentration camps. Tower, 1971, $.95 paperback.

BAUER, YEHUDAH. *Flight and Rescue: Brichah.* Story of the continual movement of refugees from the DP camps in Germany, past British blockade, into Palestine, between 1944 and 1948. Random House, 1970, $8.95.

BELL, LELAND V. *In Hitler's Shadow: The Anatomy of American Nazism.* A history of Nazism in America from its inception in the 1920's to the present. Kennikat Press, 1973, $7.95.

BERKOVITS, ELIEZER. *Faith After the Holocaust.* What is our attitude toward God and His involvement in the tragedy of European Jewry? What is His place as man confronts poverty, war, injustice? Ktav, 1973, $7.50, $4.95 paperback.

BOR, JOSEF. *The Terezin Requiem: A Narrative of the Human Spirit.* A Czech conductor rehearses and performs Verdi's *Requiem* amid the numbing horrors of Terezin concentration camp. After the last note, all are shipped to Auschwitz. Knopf, 1963, $3.50. Out of print.

BOROWSKI, THADEUSZ. *This Way to the Gas, Ladies and Gentlemen!* Auschwitz remembered in a series of short stories, where the unspeakable becomes "normal," the abnormal becomes "routine." The writer was a young Polish political prisoner who committed suicide soon after his release. Penguin Books, 1976, $2.95 paperback.

BRACHER, KARL DIETRICH. *The German Dictatorship.* Tightly written, comprehensive study of the Nazi phenomenon. Praeger, 1970, $13.95 cloth; $5.95 paperback.

BULLOCK, ALAN. *Hitler: A Study in Tyranny.* One of the earliest, and now classic, works on the topic. Harper Torch, 1971, abridged ed., $1.50 paperback; revised ed., $4.75 paperback.

COHEN, ARTHUR A., ed. *Arguments and Doctrines: A Reader of Jewish Thinking in the Aftermath of the Holocaust.* A collection of seminal essays that merit re-reading and reassessment. Jewish Publication Society and Harper & Row, 1970, $11.95.

COHN, NORMAN. *Warrant for Genocide: The Myth of the World Jewish Conspiracy and the Protocols of the Elders of Zion*—how it helped provoke massacres in Russia and how it helped prepare the way for the near-extermination of European Jewry. Harper & Row, 1967, $6.95 cloth; 1969, $2.45 paperback.

DAVIDSON, EUGENE. *The Trial of the Germans: An Account of the Twenty-Two Defendants Before the International Tribunal at Nuremberg.* Guilt, mass-murder, political aggression are examined through the bizarre case histories explored at Nuremberg. Macmillan, 1972, $3.95 paperback.

DAWIDOWICZ, LUCY. *The War Against the Jews, 1933-1945.* Deals with questions not fully covered by earlier works: Judenrat, resistance. Holt, Rinehart and Winston, 1975, $15.00; Bantam, $2.25 paperback.

DEKEL, EPHRAIM. *B'riha: Flight to the Homeland.* The organization and work of the Jewish underground movement from Europe to Palestine during and after World War II. Herzl Press, $6.95.

DONAT, ALEXANDER. *The Holocaust Kingdom.* The true story of a Jewish couple who hid their child with a Polish couple before they were deported. Holt, Rinehart and Winston, 1965, $5.95. Out of print.

ESH, SHAUL, et al., eds. *Yad VaShem Studies of the European Catastrophe and Resistance.* Essays, studies, statistics, memoirs, analysis, covering every aspect of the Holocaust. Eight volumes published to date. Yad VaShem, Jerusalem.

FACKENHEIM, EMIL L. *God's Presence in History: Jewish Affirmations and Philosophical Reflections.* One of the few attempts to come to grips with the theological implications of Auschwitz, and the traditional attitude toward the many catastrophes that have befallen Israel throughout its history. N.Y.U. Press, 1970, $5.00; Harper Torch, 1972, $2.75 paperback.

FEINGOLD, HENRY L. *The Politics of Rescue: The Roosevelt Administration and the Holocaust, 1938-1945.* Rutgers Univ. Press, 1970, $12.50.

FLINKER, MOSHE. *Young Moshe's Diary.* A re-issue of the autobiography of a Jewish boy in Nazi Europe, his spiritual torment and hopes before death in Auschwitz. Jewish Ed. Press, 1971, $4.50.

FRANK, ANNE. *The Diary of a Young Girl.* The now-classic diary of an adolescent girl hiding with her family during the occupation of Holland. Pocket Books, 1952, $1.95 paperback.

FRIEDLANDER, ALBERT H. *Leo Baeck: Teacher of Theresienstadt.* Biography of the leader of German Jewry during the Hitler years. Holt, Rinehart and Winston, 1968, $8.95.

—————————, ed. *Out of the Whirlwind: A Reader of Holocaust Literature.* U.A.H.C., 1968, text $7.50; teacher's guide $3.50 paperback.

FRIEDMAN, PHILIP. *Martyrs and Fighters: The Epic of the Warsaw Ghetto.* An anthology of original documents and eye-witness reports. Lancer Books. Out of print.

FRIEDMAN, SAUL S. *No Haven for the Oppressed: United States Policy Toward Jewish Refugees, 1938-1945.* The political machinations to which Jewish immigration was sacrificed and the unwillingness on the part of American-Jewish leadership to advocate the Jewish cause for fear of antagonizing public opinion. Wayne State Univ. Press, 1973, $15.95.

FRIEDRICH, OTTO. *Before the Deluge: A Portrait of Berlin in the 1920's.* Harper & Row, 1972, $10.00; Avon, 1973, $1.95 paperback.

GLATSTEIN, JACOB; KNOX, ISRAEL; and MARGOSHES, SAMUEL. *Anthology of Holocaust Literature.* Jewish Publication Society, 1969, $10.00; Atheneum, $4.95 paperback.

GOLDSTEIN, CHARLES. *The Bunker.* The story of seven Jews who survived the Warsaw Ghetto rebellion of 1943 and the uprising of 1944. Atheneum T-27, 1972, $3.95 paperback.

GREEN, GERALD. *The Artists of Terezin.* The advantages of "resettlement"—a library, an artists' "colony"—were shown to the Red Cross and others in this "showcase" camp. Hawthorn Books, 1970, $10.00.

GRUNBERGER, RICHARD. *The 12-Year Reich: A Social History of Nazi Germany, 1933-1945.* Indispensable for background information. Holt, Rinehart and Winston, 1971, $10.00; Ballantine, 1972, $1.95 paperback.

GRUNFELD, FREDERIC V. *The Hitler File: A Social History of the Nazis 1918-1945.* A collection of pictures and text oriented toward daily life, the arts and culture of the German people. Random House, 1974, $25.00.

HALPERIN, IRVING. *Messengers From the Dead: Literature of the Holocaust.* On the reading and writing of Holocaust literature. Westminster Press, 1970, $5.00.

HAREL, ISSER. *The House on Garibaldi Street.* The difficulties, "goofs," successes and failures of the intelligence operation that resulted in the capture of Adolph Eichman, as told by the director of that operation. Viking Press, 1975, $8.95; Bantam, $1.95 paperback.

HAUSNER, GIDEON. *Justice in Jerusalem.* The Israeli prosecutor in the Eichman Process carefully details the progress of the trial and provides historical background material. Harper & Row, 1966, $12.50. Schocken Books, 1969, $2.95 paperback.

HERSEY, JOHN. *The Wall*. A fictional work on life in the Warsaw Ghetto patterned after the diaries found in the ruins of the ghetto after the war. The narrator is a diarist whose objective is to present a view of life in which nothing is forgotten—ever. Knopf, 1950, $8.95; Bantam, $2.25 paperback.

HILBERG, RAOUL. *Documents of Destruction: Germany and Jewry, 1933-1945*. A collection of documents from German government files. Primary source materials. Quadrangle QP-311, 1971, $3.95 paperback.

HOCHHUTH, RALPH. *The Deputy*. A play about the attitude of Pope Pius XII and the Catholic Church toward the Nazi persecution of the Jews. Grove Press B-154, 1964, $2.45.

HOLLY, DAVID. *Exodus, 1947*. The story of the Haganah ship loaded with refugees, intercepted by the British navy. Little, Brown, 1969, $6.95.

JACOT, MICHAEL. *The Last Butterfly*. A comedian so weighted down by sadness that he can no longer make people laugh is arrested by the Nazis and forced to entertain children whose parents have been gassed in Auschwitz. Bobbs-Merrill, 1964, $6.95; Ballantine Books, 1975, $1.50 paperback.

Jewish Resistance During the Holocaust: Proceedings of the Conference on Manifestations of Jewish Resistance. April 7-11, 1968. Yad VaShem, Jerusalem.

JOFFROY, PIERRE. *A Spy for God: The Ordeal of Kurt Gerstein*. He knew of the gas chambers and the Zyklon B, but no one believed him. Gerstein's fate was brought to attention in *The Deputy*. Grosset & Dunlap UL-2, 1972, $2.95.

KANTOR, ALFRED. *The Book of Alfred Kantor*. A collection of watercolors based on sketches made in the camps. McGraw-Hill, 1971, $17.95.

KATSH, ABRAHAM, ed. *The Warsaw Diary of Chaim Kaplan*. Covers the period September, 1939—August, 1942. A cumulative record of Nazi horror and of Jewish life in the doomed community. Macmillan, 1973, $6.95; $2.95 paperback.

KATZ, ROBERT. *Black Sabbath*. Jewish fate in Italy after the Fascist take-over. Macmillan, 1969, $7.95.

KLARSFELD, BEATE. *Wherever They May Be: One Woman's Battle Against Nazism*. First person account of a German-Protestant woman, one of the most famous activists against Nazi war criminals. Vanguard Press, 1975, $10.00.

KLUGER, RUTH, and MANN, PEGGY. *The Last Escape*. The launching of the largest secret rescue movement of all times. This first-person novel tells the true story with impact and suspense. Doubleday, 1973, $10.00; Pinnacle Books, 1974, $1.95 paperback.

KOGON, EUGEN. *The Theory and Practice of Hell*. The SS and the concentration camp system are described by a survivor. Octagon, 1972 reprint, $12.00; Berkley Pub., $1.25 paperback.

KOLITZ, ZVI. *Survival for What?* Essays on the Jewish *neshamah*, Israel, the Holocaust. Includes "Yossel Rakover Speaks to God." Philosophical Library, $6.50.

KORMAN, GERD. *Hunter and Hunted: Human History of the Holocaust*. An anthology dealing with several stages of the Holocaust: refugee crisis of the 1930's to liberation in 1945. Includes citations from the testimony before the Congressional Committee on Immigration on the admission of German refugee children held in May, 1939. Viking, 1973, $8.95; Delta, $2.95 paperback.

KOSINSKI, JERZY. *The Painted Bird*. A dark-haired, olive-skinned boy is abandoned by his parents during the war and wanders from village to village. Modern Library, 1970 reprint, $3.95; Bantam, $1.75 paperback.

KOVALY, HEDA, and KOHAK, ERAZIM. *The Victors and the Vanquished*. Stalinist Russia and occupied Czechoslovakia after the war. Horizon Press, 1973, $8.95.

KURZMAN, DAN. *The Race for Rome*. The Allied armies race for Rome while the Nazis threaten to destroy the city. Extensive treatment of the fate of the city's Jewish population. Doubleday, 1975, $10.00.

LANGER, LAWRENCE L. *The Holocaust and the Literary Imagination.* An investigation of the aesthetic metamorphoses and the efforts of modern writers to confront the reality of the Holocaust. Yale Univ. Press, 1975, $12.50.

LANGER, WALTER C. *The Mind of Adolf Hitler.* A secret war report gathered by military intelligence. Basic Books, 1972, $12.00; N.A.L., 1973, $1.50 paperback.

LEVI, PRIMO. *Survival in Auschwitz: The Nazi Assault on Humanity.* Memoir of Auschwitz by an Italian intellectual. A monument to the indestructibility of the human spirit. Macmillan, 1961, $1.25 paperback.

LEVIN, NORA. *The Holocaust: The Destruction of European Jewry, 1933-1945.* Rejects passivity theory by describing Jewish resistance to a greater degree than is commonly known. Schocken, 1973, $7.95 paperback.

LEWY, GUNTHER. *The Catholic Church and Nazi Germany.* The best study of the response of the Pope and the German Catholic Church to the Holocaust. McGraw-Hill, 1964, $1.95 paperback.

LIPTZIN, SOLOMON C. *Germany's Stepchildren.* Biographies of famous Jewish-German personalities from the Enlightenment to the Nazi era investigate the tragic duality in the Jewish soul vis-a-vis the majority culture. Books for Libraries, reprint of the 1944 edition, $14.50.

LUSTIG, ARNOST. *A Prayer for Katerina Horovitzova.* A powerful novel of concentration camp experience by a survivor. Harper & Row, 1973, $5.95; Avon, $1.50 paperback.

MARK, BER. *Uprising in the Warsaw Ghetto.* A chronologically arranged narrative and a collection of relevant documents. Schocken Books, 1975, $8.95 hardbound; $3.45 paperback.

MASTERS, ANTHONY. *The Summer That Bled: The Biography of Hannah Senesh.* Hannah Senesh was one of a group of Jewish parachutists dropped over Hungary in a suicide mission to rescue her people. References to Joel Brand and Resl Kastner, whose job it was to bargain with Eichman—Jews in exchange for Allied trucks. St. Martin's Press, 1973, $7.95; Pocket Books, 1974, $1.65.

MORSE, ARTHUR. *While Six Million Died.* A chronicle of American apathy and acquiescence in the genocide of Jews during World War II. Hart, 1963, $4.95 paperback.

MOSSE, GEORGE L. *Germans and Jews: An Investigation into the Roots of German Anti-Semitism.* Describes the forces that sought a unified political system based upon absolute values rather than risk Marxism or bourgeois society. Grosset & Dunlap UL—257, 1971, $2.95 paperback.

NOLTE, ERNST. *Three Faces of Fascism.* A study of the major fascist movements of the 1930's: Action Francaise, Italian Fascism, and National Socialism. N.A.L., 1969, $1.95 paperback.

PAYNE, ROBERT. *The Life and Death of Adolf Hitler.* Popular Library, 1973, $1.95.

POLIAKOV, LEON. *Harvest of Hate: The Nazi Program for the Destruction of the Jews in Europe.* A history of the final solution. Greenwood, 1971, reprint of 1954 ed., $13.00.

—————————. *The Aryan Myth: A History of Racist and Nationalist Ideas in Europe.* Basic Books, 1974, $12.00.

PRESSER, JACOB. *The Destruction of the Dutch Jews.* Not only a record of the destruction of the Jews, but of the progressive corruption of a "good" society without whose cooperation the Nazi timetable might have proceeded less smoothly. Dutton, 1969, $10.00.

RECK-MALLECZEWEN, FRIEDERICH P. *Diary of a Man in Despair.* The words of an intellectual and aristocrat, shot by the Gestapo in February, 1945. Macmillan, 1972, $1.95.

REITLINGER, GERALD. *The Final Solution*. A comprehensive history. A. S. Barnes, 1961 rev. ed., $2.45 paperback.

—————————. *SS—Alibi of a Nation, 1922-45*. History, organization, role of the SS as fighting organization, Praetorian guard, and concentration camp butchers. Viking-Compass, 1957, $7.95.

ROBINSON, JACOB. *The Holocaust and After: Sources and Literature in English*. A listing of books, articles, filmstrips in English and capsule reviews of foreign language material. Keter, 1973, $20.00.

RUBENSTEIN, RICHARD L. *After Auschwitz: Essays in Contemporary Judaism*. A collection of significant essays on the death of God, the Holocaust, and modern Judaism. Bobbs-Merrill, 1966, $4.25 paperback.

—————————. *The Cunning of History: Mass Death and Contemporary Society*. Mass death and wholesale disaster as expressions of suppressed religious values. Harper & Row, 1975, $7.95.

RUTHERFORD, WARD. *Genocide: The Jews in Europe, 1930-45*. A concise, illustrated history of the well-known facts. Ballantine, 1973, $2.00.

SCHOENBERNER, GERHARD. *The Yellow Star*. A pictorial documentation. Bantam Books, 1973, $1.95.

SCHWARTZ-BART, ANDRE. *The Last of the Just*. Overwhelming novel of the Holocaust, using the theme of the 36 Just Souls by whose merit the world continues to exist. Atheneum, 1973, $3.95; Bantam, $1.95 paperback.

SHABBETAI, K. *As Sheep to the Slaughter—The Myth of Cowardice*. An impassioned statement to discredit the myth of Jewish cowardice under the Nazis. Bergen Belsen Memorial Press, 1963, $1.50 paperback.

SHIRER, WILLIAM L. *The Rise and Fall of the Third Reich: A History of Nazi Germany*. Simon & Schuster, 1960, $12.50 cloth; Fawcett, $1.95 paperback.

SIEGEL, SEYMOUR. "Theological Reflections on the Destruction of European Jewry." *Conservative Judaism*, Vol. 16, No. 4, Summer, 1964.

SLOAN, JACOB, editor and translator. *Notes from the Warsaw Ghetto: The Journal of Emanuel Ringelblum.* The notes and diaries of Emanuel Ringelblum which were dug up from the rubble of the Warsaw Ghetto. Schocken Books, 1975 reprint, $4.50 paperback.

SMITH, MARCUS J. *The Harrowing of Hell: Dachau.* One of the first Americans to enter Dachau after it was liberated, the author was a medical officer charged with caring for the 32,000 starving prisoners. Univ. of New Mexico Press, 1972, $6.95.

STEINBERG, LUCIEN. *Not As a Lamb.* Evidence of Jewish resistance to present threat against the canard of submissiveness. Atheneum, 1974, $12.50.

STEINBERG, MILTON. *A Partisan Guide to the Jewish Problem.* A famous rabbi stirs his people to new life in the aftermath of death and Holocaust, general apathy and renewed dispersion. Charter Books, 1949, $2.95.

STEINER, GEORGE. *In Bluebeard's Castle: Some Notes Toward the Redefinition of Culture.* Lectures on 20th-century middle-European culture provide important background analysis of the Holocaust phenomenon. Yale Univ. Press, 1974, $1.95.

——————————. *Language and Silence: Essays on Language, Literature and the Inhuman.* Atheneum, $3.95 paperback.

SUHL, YURI. *They Fought Back: The Story of the Jewish Resistance in Nazi Europe.* A distinguished writer offers previously unavailable evidence that Resistance groups existed throughout Europe in almost every ghetto and concentration camp. Schocken, 1975, $4.50 paperback.

THALMAN, RITA, and FEINERMAN, EMMANUEL. *Crystal Night: 9-10 November, 1938.* Documented narrative of the first mass outrage against the total Jewish community in Germany. Coward McCann, 1974, $5.95.

THOMAS, GORDON, and WITTS, MAX. *Voyage of the Damned.* The refugee ship *St. Louis,* turned away from Cuba and refused entry to the U.S., returns to Germany. Stein & Day, $8.95; Fawcett, 1975, $1.75 paperback.

TILLION, GERMAINE. *Ravensbruck.* An eyewitness account of the notorious concentration camp for women, by an inmate from 1942-45. Anchor A-1013, 1975, $2.95 paperback.

TRUNK, ISAIAH. *Judenrat: The Jewish Councils in Eastern Europe Under Nazi Occupation.* Why and how the councils worked—their difficult role in the destruction of European Jewry. Macmillan, 1972, $14.95.

TUSHNET, LEONARD. *The Pavement of Hell.* An exploration of the moral choices of the leaders of the Judenrat, the Jewish councils under Nazi occupation. St. Martin's Press, 1973, $7.95.

URIS, LEON. *Mila 18.* The title is the address of the headquarters of the Jewish resistance in the Warsaw ghetto. The story of the revolt in novelistic form. Doubleday, 1961, $6.95; Bantam, 1970, $1.75 paperback.

VIERECK, PETER. *Metapolitics: The Roots of the Nazi Mind.* The antecedents of Nazi philosophy and anti-Semitism in German romantic poetry, music and social thought. Capricorn, 1961, $2.85 paperback.

VOLAVKOVA, HANA. *I Never Saw Another Butterfly.* A unique collection of drawings by children in the Terezin concentration camp. McGraw-Hill, 1964, $4.95.

WEINREICH, MAX. *Hitler's Professors: The Part of Scholarship in Germany's Crimes Against the Jewish People.* Scientists, sociologists, philosophers, historians and medical experimenters, all in step with the dictatorship. YIVO, 1946, $5.00.

WEISS, PETER. *The Investigation.* A play set in a German court twenty years after the Holocaust, where 21 people are on trial for mass murder. Atheneum, 1966, $3.95 paperback.

WIESEL, ELIE. *Night. Dawn. The Accident.* One-volume edition of three of Wiesel's seminal novels. Hill & Wang, 1972, $7.95. Wiesel's books are available in paperback from Avon.

—————————. *The Town Beyond the Wall.* Winner of 1965 Fiction Award by the Jewish Book Council. Story of Michael, a young survivor of the Holocaust, who decides to return to the town behind the Iron Curtain from which he came. Holt, Rinehart and Winston, 1964, $4.95; Avon, 1969, $1.25 paperback.

—————————. *One Generation After.* Essays on the aftermath of the Holocaust. Random, 1970, $5.95; Avon, 1971, $1.25 paperback.

WIESENTHAL, SIMON. *The Murderers Among Us.* Memoirs of the famous Nazi-hunter. Bantam Books, 1973, $1.25 paperback.

WYKES, ALAN. *Heydrich.* A brief biography of the "Butcher of Prague," the man first entrusted to implement the "Final Solution." Ballantine Books, 1973, $1.50.

ISRAEL, ZIONISM AND THE MIDDLE EAST

BAUER, YEHUDA. *From Diplomacy to Resistance.* A history of Jewish Palestine during World War II. Atheneum, 1973, $4.65 paperback.

Bazak Guide to Israel 1975-76. The favorite among guides, newly revised and with a special 48-page restaurant guide. Harper & Row, 1975, $5.95.

BEGIN, MENACHEM. *The Revolt: The Story of the Irgun.* The book opens in a Soviet prison camp in Siberia in 1940 and closes with the birth of the State of Israel. The history of the Jewish underground army written by its commander-in-chief. Nash Publ., 1972, $7.95.

BEN-GURION, DAVID. *Israel, A Personal History.* A history of the modern State of Israel. Funk & Wagnalls, 1971, $20.00.

——————. *The Jews in Their Land.* A history of the land of Israel from the Biblical period to the present day by well-known scholars. Illustrated. Doubleday, 1974, $9.95.

BOKSER, BEN ZION. *Jews, Judaism and the State of Israel.* The significance of Judaism's unique stress on religion, people, and land. Herzl Press, 1974, $6.95.

BUBER, MARTIN. *Israel and the World: Essays in a Time of Crisis.* The relation of Jewish thinking to contemporary intellectual movements. Schocken, 1948, $2.95.

——————. *On Zion: The History of an Idea.* A sensitively written history of the idea and the men who carried it forward. Schocken, 1973, $7.00.

——————. *Paths in Utopia.* On socialism, community, Zionism. Beacon Press, 1948, $3.95 paperback.

COLLINS, LARRY, and LAPIERRE, DOMINIQUE. *O Jerusalem.* Exciting account of the battle for Jerusalem, 1947-48. Pocket Books, 1973, $1.95.

CRIDEN, YOSEF, and GELB, SAADIA. *The Kibbutz Experience: Dialogue in*

Kfar Blum. Two American kibbutzniks discuss the ideals and problems of kibbutz life. Herzl Press, 1974, $7.95; Schocken, $3.45 paperback.

DAVIS, MOSHE, ed. *Yom Kippur War: Israel and the Jewish People.* A collection of articles by scholars and men of action reflecting attitudes about the war and its aftermath. Arno Press, 1974, $9.00.

EBAN, ABBA. *My Country.* The history of the State of Israel from its founding to the Six-Day War. The impact of immigration, economic development, and cultural advances during 25 years of independence. Photo illustrated. Random House, 1972, $15.00.

ELDAD, ISRAEL. *The Jewish Revolution: Jewish Statehood.* A bold, militant advocacy of Zionism. Israel must learn to rely on its own forces, spiritual and military. Shengold, 1971, $5.95.

ELON, AMOS. *The Israelis: Founders and Sons.* An analysis of Israel's social, cultural, and political life. Bantam, 1972, $1.95 paperback.

FEIN, LEONARD. *Politics in Israel.* A useful analysis of the internal workings of Israel's political system. Little, Brown, 1967, $3.95 paperback.

Fodor's Israel 1975. A revised and updated edition of the famous guidebook. David McKay, 1975, $8.95.

GERVASI, FRANK. *The Case for Israel.* A fully-documented account of the events which led up to three wars with the Arabs, told by a non-Jew who would urge the Arabs to recognize the reality of Israel's legitimate permanency in the region. Viking Press, 1967, $5.50; Compass, $1.95 paperback.

——————. *Thunder over the Mediterranean.* A first-hand study of the Yom Kippur War and its relationship to the Middle East. David McKay, 1975, $8.50.

GILBERT, MARTIN. *Atlas of the Arab-Israeli Conflict.* Visual narrative in 101 maps. Macmillan, 1975, $6.95.

GOITEIN, SOLOMON D. *Jews and Arabs: Their Contacts Through the Ages.* A deep insight into the long, complex history of Arab-Jewish relations. Schocken, 1964, 1967, $3.45 paperback.

GOLDBERG, ISRAEL. (Learsi) *Fulfillment: The Epic Story of Zionism.* Comprehensive history of the Zionist movement from its beginnings to the establishment of the State of Israel. Herzl Press, 1951, reprinted 1972, $4.95 paperback.

GOLDSTEIN, ISRAEL. *Israel At Home and Abroad.* A panorama of contemporary Jewish life throughout the world. A treasury of information on Zionist, Jewish, and universal themes. Bloch, 1973, $6.95.

GORKIN, MICHAEL. *Border Kibbutz.* A young American Jew tells of his life on a kibbutz—an appraisal of life under threat of annihilation. Hart, 1973, $2.45.

GROUSSARD, SERGE. *The Blood of Israel.* A factual account of the massacre of the Israeli athletes at the 1972 Munich Olympics. William Morrow, 1975, $12.50.

HART, HAROLD. *Yom Kippur Plus 100 Days.* Day-by-day events in Israel during and after the war chronicled by items selected from the Jerusalem Post. Hart Publ. Co., 1974, $8.95.

HAUER, CHRISTIAN E. *Crisis and Conscience in the Middle East.* A Protestant theologian and educator defends Israel. Quadrangle, 1970, $5.95.

HECKELMAN, A. JOSEPH. *American Volunteers in Israel's War of Independence, 1947-1949.* The key events in the War of Independence, in which many foreign volunteers participated and many gave their lives. Ktav, 1974, $12.50.

HERTZBERG, ARTHUR. *The Zionist Idea: A Historical Analysis and Reader.* An anthology. Atheneum, 1959, $5.95 paperback.

HERZOG, CHAIM. *The War of Atonement, 1973.* Analysis of military aspects of the war and its influence upon present trends and alignments, by the former head of Israeli military intelligence. Little, Brown, 1975, $10.00.

HESCHEL, ABRAHAM JOSHUA. *Israel: An Echo of Eternity.* The significance of Israel for Jews and the world. Farrar, Straus & Giroux, 1969, $5.50; Noonday, 1969, $2.95 paperback.

HOLTZ, AVRAHAM, ed. *The Holy City: Jews on Jerusalem.* Passages from Jewish literature illuminating the unique relationship between the Jewish people and the Holy City. Viking Press, 1971, $6.00.

HUREWITZ, JACOB. *Struggle for Palestine.* An authoritative, documented account of the crucial 1939-49 era. Greenwood, 1968, reprint of 1950 edition, $16.00.

The Israel Pocket Library. A series of books containing material originally published in the *Encyclopedia Judaica.* Available: Anti-Semitism; Archaeology of the Holy Land; Geography of Israel; History of Israel Until 1880; Jerusalem; Zionism. Forthcoming: Culture of Israel; Democracy in Israel; Education and Science in Israel; Economy of Israel; History of Israel from 1880; Holocaust; Immigration and Settlement; Religious Life in Israel; Society of Israel. Two Continents Publ./Keter Books, $1.95 and $2.50.

KURZMAN, DAN. *Genesis 1948: The First Arab-Israeli War.* An exciting chronicle. N.A.L. Signet, 1972, $1.95.

LAQUEUR, WALTER. *A History of Zionism.* The most complete, well-documented one-volume history of Zionism. Holt, Rinehart and Winston, 1972, $10.00; Schocken, $6.95 paperback.

——————————, ed. *The Israel-Arab Reader: A Documentary History of the Middle East.* Zionist and Arab points of view as well as a history of their grievances. Bantam, 1970, $2.95 paperback.

——————————. *The Road to War: The Origin and Aftermath of the Arab-Israeli Conflict, 1967-68.* Penguin, 1969, $1.75 paperback. Out of print.

LUCAS, NOAH. *A Modern History of Israel.* Praeger, 1975, $20.00.

LUTTWAK, EDWARD, and HOROWITZ, DAN. *The Israeli Army.* Combines history, strategy, technology, leadership psychology, logistics into a well-rounded portrait. Harper & Row, 1975, $15.00.
Related titles: ALLON, YIGAL. *Shield of David: The Story of Israel's Armed Forces,* Random House, 1970, $10.00; SCHIFF, ZEEV, *A History of the Israeli Army, 1870-1974,* Straight Arrow, 1974, $19.95.

NAAMANI, ISRAEL T.; RUDAVSKY, DAVID; and KATSH, ABRAHAM, eds. *Israel: Its Politics and Philosophy.* Israel in the words of its leaders, who provide a broad spectrum of opinions. An anthology of speeches and essays. Behrman House, 1973, $4.95 paperback.

OESTERREICHER, JOHN, and SINAI, ANNE, eds. *Jerusalem.* Prepared under auspices of the American Academic Association for Peace in the Middle East. Anthology on Jerusalem: its history, its people, and its meaning to Jews, Christians and Moslems. John Jay, 1974, $4.95 paperback.

ORNI, EPHRAIM, and EFRAT, ELISHA. *Geography of Israel.* A revised edition of the standard reference book. Jewish Publication Society, 1973, $10.95.

PATAI, RAPHAEL. *The Arab Mind.* Traditions of Arab society and their effects on social and political behavior. Scribner's, 1973, $12.50; $5.45 paperback.

———. *Israel Between East and West.* A study in human relations between Oriental and Western Jews in Israel today. Greenwood Press, 1970, $12.00.

PEDAHZUR, DAVID, ed. *Israel 25: A Pictorial Celebration.* 325 photographs celebrate the founders, builders, and defenders of Israel. Includes messages by Golda Meir, Ben Gurion and others. Arlington House, 1973, $17.95.

POSTAL, BERNARD, and LEVY, HENRY W. *And the Hills Shouted for Joy: The Day Israel Was Born.* Thirteen days in May, 1948, against a background of international politics, sabotage, threat of annihilation, and Jewish courage and heroism. David McKay, 1973, $8.95.

ISRAEL, ZIONISM AND THE MIDDLE EAST

RUBINSTEIN, ARYEH. *The Return to Zion.* A brief history of aliyah and settlement in the land of Israel. Many photographs. Leon Amiel, 1974, $3.95.

SACHAR, HOWARD M. *The Emergence of the Middle East, 1914-1924.* The collapse of the Ottoman Empire and the efforts of the great powers of Europe as a result of that power vacuum; the emergence of un-suspected national ambitions and alignments. Knopf, 1969, $12.50.

——————. *Europe Leaves the Middle East (1936-1956).* Volume II in the author's history of the Modern State of Israel. World War II and the post-war years as they affected the Jewish state. Alfred A. Knopf, 1972, $15.00.

SCHOENBRUN, DAVID, and SZEKELY, ROBERT and LUCY. *The New Israelis.* A composite portrait of the first generation born in Israel. Atheneum, 1973, $7.95.

SCHWEID, ELIEZER. *Israel at the Crossroads.* Focuses upon relations between Israel and the Diaspora, between religious and non-religious Jews in Israel, and the relationship of various movements within modern Judaism to the Jewish tradition. Jewish Publication Society, 1973, $5.95.

SHAPIRA AVRAHAM, ed. *The Seventh Day: Soldiers Talk About the Six-Day War (1967).* Talks recorded and edited by a group of young kibbutz members about the moral problems of war. Scribner's, 1972, $2.45 paperback.

SHARON, ARIEH. *Planning Jerusalem.* The plan for renewing the old city of Jerusalem and its environs. McGraw-Hill, 1973, $25.00.

SILBERG, MOSHE. *Talmudic Law and the Modern State.* A member of Israel's Supreme Court assesses the special relevance of Talmudic law to the problems of the State of Israel. Burning Bush Press, 1973, $7.95.

SILVERBERG, ROBERT. *If I Forget Thee, O Jerusalem.* The birth of the State and the role American Jews played in its creation. Pyramid Books, 1972, $1.95 paperback.

SINGER, HOWARD. *Bring Forth the Mighty Men: On Violence and the Jewish Character.* War reportage of the 1967 War is the basis for an exploration of this topic. Funk & Wagnalls, 1969, $6.95.

SLATER, LEONARD. *The Pledge.* The participation of Americans and other Western Jews in smuggling arms and munitions into Israel during the War of Independence. Pocket Books, 1971, $1.50 paperback.

SPIRO, MELFORD. *Kibbutz: Venture in Utopia.* An established and standard work on collective settlement in Israel. Revised and updated. Harvard Univ. Press, HP-82, new edition 1975, $3.95 paperback; Schocken, 1971, $2.75.

——————. and SPIRO, AUDREY. *Children of the Kibbutz: A Study in Child Training and Personality.* How does a child raised by the community differ from one growing up in a nuclear family? Revised and updated. Harvard Univ. Press, HP-83, 1975, $4.95.

TALMON, YONINA. *Family and Community in the Kibbutz.* Essays on the individual and the family in an egalitarian communal society. Harvard Univ. Press, 1972, $3.75 paperback.

TIGER, LIONEL, and SHEPHER, JOSEPH. *Women in the Kibbutz.* Women at home and in public life. Harcourt Brace, 1975, $10.00.

VILNAY, ZEV. *Legends of Jerusalem.* Over 300 legends of Judaism, Christianity and Islam concerning sites in the Holy City. Jewish Publication Society, 1973, $6.95.

ZUCKER, NORMAN L. *The Coming Crisis in Israel: Private Faith and Public Policy.* The ongoing conflict between the government and the Rabbinate; the electoral system; control over marriage, divorce and the definition of who is a Jew. M.I.T. Press, 1973, $10.00.

BAUM, CHARLOTTE; HYMAN, PAULA; and MICHEL, SONYA. *The Jewish Woman in America.* Her experience, image, reality, and response to Jewish and American culture. Dial Press, 1975, $8.95.

BERKOVITS, ELIEZER. *Crisis and Faith.* A major statement on the crises facing Judaism today and what our responses should be. Included are such personal problems as sexual ethics, divorce, and conversion, as well as an examination of Israel's crisis of spiritual survival in an age of moral decline. Hebrew Publishing Co., 1975, $8.50.

BIRMINGHAM, STEPHEN. *Our Crowd.* Jewish families of New York and how they became great. Harper & Row, 1967, $12.50.

————————. *The Grandees.* The development of America's Sephardic elite. Harper & Row, 1971, $12.50.

BLAU, JOSEPH L., and BARON, SALO W. *The Jews of the United States 1790-1840.* A collection of private and public documents which intimately portray the character of the Jews in early America. 3 vols. Jewish Publication Society, 1964, $30.00 a set.

BOROWITZ, EUGENE B. *The Mask Jews Wear.* (See listing under *Jewish Identity.*)

BRICKMAN, WILLIAM W. *The Jewish Community in America.* An annotated and classified bibliographic guide with an introductory essay placing the community into perspective. Burt Franklin, 1974, $13.50.

CAHAN, ABRAHAM, tr. by Stein, Leon, et al. *The Education of Abraham Cahan.* The first two of five volumes of Cahan's autobiography, "Bleter Fun Mein Leben," in translation, from his birth in 1860 to the start of his literary and journalistic career in America in 1890. Jewish Publication Society, 1969, $7.50.

————————. *The Rise of David Levinsky.* 1917 classic about the rise of a Russian Jewish immigrant in New York's garment industry.Harper & Row, 1960, $3.95.

CHYET, STANLEY, ed. *Lives and Voices: A Collection of 19th and 20th Century American Jewish Memoirs.* Jewish Publication Society, 1972, $6.50.

COHEN, NAOMI W. *Not Free to Desist: The American-Jewish Committee, 1906-1966.* A history of the defense organization and its involvement in Jewish social and cultural life in the United States and abroad. Jewish Publication Society, 1972, $9.00.

DAVIS, MOSHE. *The Emergence of Conservative Judaism.* A history of Judaism in the United States with basic information on the development of Conservative Judaism. Jewish Publication Society 1963, $5.50.

DIAMOND, SANDER A. *The Nazi Movement in the United States, 1924-1941.* A detailed history of the movement. Cornell University Press, 1973, $15.00.

DINNERSTEIN, LEONARD, and PALSSON, MARY D., eds. *Jews in the South.* This comprehensive anthology examines various aspects of Jewish life in the South from colonial times to the present. Louisiana State University Press, 1973, $12.50.

ELOVITZ, MARK H. *A Century of Jewish Life in Dixie: The Birmingham Experience.* The history of the Jewish community of Birmingham as a paradigm of Jewish experience in America. Univ. of Alabama Press, 1975, $10.00.

FISHMAN, HERTZEL. *American Protestantism and the Jewish State.* This study traces the important role played both by American Protestants and by Protestant theology in the formation of American policy towards Israel. Wayne State Univ. Press, 1973, $11.95.

FISHMAN, PRISCILLA, ed. *The Jews of the United States.* A survey of all aspects of American Jewish life, largely based upon materials contained in the Encyclopedia Judaica. Quadrangle, 1973, $8.95.

FRIEDMAN, LEE M. *Jewish Pioneers and Patriots.* A miscellany of essays on

Jewish interaction with American society, presidents, and among themselves. Jewish Publication Society, 1955.

GLAZER, NATHAN. *American Judaism,* 2nd ed. A revised and updated study of the history, institutions, sociology and thought of American Jewry. University of Chicago, 1957, $5.95 text edition, $2.95 paperback.

HAPGOOD, HUTCHINS. *The Spirit of the Ghetto: Studies in the Jewish Quarter of New York.* An eyewitness description of a community of immigrants, workers in sweatshops, intellectuals, revolutionaries, trade-unionists and Talmudists in 1902. Schocken Books SB-128, 1966, $2.45.

HIMMELFARB, MILTON. *The Jews of Modernity.* Most of these essays appeared in *Commentary* magazine. They deal with the tension which exists between tradition and modernity, particularism and universalism, messianic politics, intellectuals and bourgeois—all concerns of the modern American Jewish community. Basic Books, 1973, $10.95.

HIRSCHFELD, FRITZ. *Colonial Jews and American Independence.* How Jews brought to the struggle for American liberty their own struggle for their rights as first class citizens. Dodd-Mead, 1975, $10.00.

HOWE, IRVING. *World of Our Fathers.* Harcourt Brace Jovanovich, 1976, $14.95.

KAHANE, RABBI MEIR. *The Story of the Jewish Defense League.* The story of the militant Jewish Defense League, written by its founder. Chilton Book Co., 1975, $7.95.

——————————. *Time to Go Home.* The author advocates that American Jews emigrate to Israel. Nash Publ., 1973, $7.95.

KAHN, ROGER. *The Passionate People: What It Means to Be a Jew in America.* A composite portrait of the American Jew. Wm. Morrow & Co., 1968, $6.95.

KAPLAN, MORDECAI M. *The Future of the American Jew.* Kaplan's naturalist, pragmatic religious philosophy underlies his understanding of Jewish identity and serves as the rationale for his program for a reconstruction of Jewish life in America. Reconstructionist Press, 1948, $2.95 paperback.

KARP, ABRAHAM. *The Jewish Experience in America.* 5 volumes. Selected studies from the publications of the American Jewish Historical Society. Edited and with an introduction by Abraham J. Karp. Ktav, 1969, $49.50.

KORN, BERTRAM. *American Jewry and the Civil War.* Documentary history of the Jewish response to and participation in the Civil War. Atheneum, 1970, $4.50 paperback.

LANDMAN, LEO, ed. *Judaism and Drugs.* A collection of essays by recognized scholars representing various viewpoints: history, Halachah, psychology and sociology. Sepher-Hermon Press, 1973, $5.95.

LEBESON, ANITA. *Pilgrim People.* One of the best volumes in form, content, and lively writing on American Jewry. Minerva Press, 1950, $3.95.

LEVINE, NAOMI, and HOCHBAUM, MARTIN. *Poor Jews: An American Awakening.* Essays exploring instances of poverty within Jewish communities. Transaction, 1974, $3.95.

LIEBMAN, CHARLES S. *The Ambivalent American Jew.* Analysis of the tensions affecting the American Jew caught between a desire to integrate into American society and a felt need for the survival of the Jewish group. Jewish Publication Society, 1973, $5.95.

MARCUS, JACOB R. *American Jewry: Documents, Eighteenth Century.* A vivid picture of the life of the 18th century American Jew is presented through the medium of contemporary documents. HUC Press and Ktav, 1958, $8.50.

——————————. *The Colonial American Jew, 1492-1776.* A fascinating history of the earliest American Jews. Wayne State University, 1970, 3 vols., $45.00.

—————————. *Critical Studies in American Jewish History.* Selected studies from the publications of the American Jewish Archives. Ktav, 1971, 3 vols., $27.50.

—————————. *Early American Jewry.* 2 vols.: I. The Jews of New York, New England, and Canada 1649-1794; II. The Jews of Pennsylvania and the South 1655-1790. Ktav, 1975, $35.00.

—————————. *Memoirs of American Jews 1775-1865.* Autobiographical writings by famous Jewish Americans. Primary sources. Out of print. Ktav, 1975, 3 vols.

METZKER, ISAAC. *The Bintel Brief.* "Letters To The Editor" of the Jewish Daily Forward sent by the Jewish immigrants on the Lower East Side of New York provide a vivid image of their lives and problems. Ballantine, 1971, $1.25.

NEUSNER, JACOB. *American Judaism: Adventure in Modernity.* A first-rate study of the conflict between classical Judaism and contemporary life in America. Prentice-Hall, 1972, $3.75 paperback.

—————————. *Contemporary Jewish Fellowship, in Theory and in Practice.* Papers on "Havurot" and unstructured synagogue groups. Ktav, 1972, $12.50.

POLL, SOLOMON. *The Hassidic Community of Williamsburg: A Study in the Sociology of Religion.* A study of social and economic aspects. Schocken Books, 1969, $3.45 paperback.

REZNECK, SAMUEL. *Unrecognized Patriots: The Jews in the American Revolution.* Contributions early Americans made to society and the legacy they left to succeeding generations. Greenwood Press, 1975, $13.95.

RIBALOW, HAROLD U. *Autobiographies of American Jews.* A cross-section of perceptions of key American Jewish figures of the last 100 years.

Jewish Publication Society, 1965, $6.00.

RIESMAN, DAVID. *Individualism Reconsidered, and Other Essays.* A collection of essays on preserving one's individuality within the Lonely Crowd and hopefully remaining impervious to its pressures. Free Press, 1954, $2.45 paperback.

RISCHIN, MOSES. *The Promised City: New York's Jews, 1870-1914.* The documented description of New York Jewry. Harvard University Press, 1962.

ROSE, PETER. *The Ghetto and Beyond: Essays on Jewish Life in America.* Random House, 1969, $4.95 paperback.

SAFRAN, NADAV. *The United States and Israel.* Cambridge, Harvard Univ. Press, 1963, $8.50.

SANDERS, RONALD. *The Downtown Jews: Portraits of an Immigrant Generation.* The story of the Americanization of the Jewish immigrants is organized around the life of Abraham Cahan, the editor of the Jewish Daily Forward. Harper & Row, 1969, $10.00.

SCHAPPES, MORRIS U., ed. *Documentary History of the Jews in the United States, 1654-1875.* A treasury of historic documents depicting the role of the Jewish people from Colonial times to 1875. Schocken, 1971, $12.50 cloth, $6.95 paperback.

SCHOENER, ALLON, ed. *Portal to America: The Lower East Side, 1870-1925.* Pictorial remembrances with text depicting everyday life on New York's Lower East Side when it was the center of Jewish life. Holt, Rinehart and Winston, 1972, $5.95 paperback.

SELZER, MICHAEL, ed. *"Kike!"—An Anthology of Anti-Semitism.* A documentary history in words and pictures from the Dutch colonialists to the KKK. In the same series: "Wop!" and "Chink!". N.A.L. Meridian, 1972, $3.95 paperback.

SHAPIRO, YONATHAN. *The Leadership of the American Zionist Organization, 1897-1930.* A combination of sociology and history in analyzing

Brandeis' role in shaping early American Zionism. University of Illinois Press, 1971, $9.50.

SHERMAN, BEZALEL. *The Jew Within American Society: A Study in Ethnic Individuality*. A study of Jewish life in America, focusing on the unusual "staying-power" of the Jews among American ethnic groups. Wayne State University Press, 1965, $2.50 paperback.

SIDORSKY, DAVID, ed. *The Future of the Jewish Community in America*. Prominent Jewish sociologists, scholars and community leaders address themselves to the questions of ideology, demography, the future of Jewish institutions, and education. Basic Books, 1973, $11.95.

SIEGEL, SEYMOUR. *Religion and Social Action*. The relationship between religious values and social action, and the particular contribution which religion-directed efforts can make to the solution of social problems. Published in one pamphlet with Siegel's "The Nature and Meaning of Jewish Law." Jewish Theological Seminary of America, 1963.

SKLARE, MARSHALL. *America's Jews*. A useful sociological survey of American Jewry examining its origins and experiences, the cultural patterns and intergroup relations. Random House, 1972, $3.15 paperback.

————. *Conservative Judaism: An American Religious Movement*. The history of the movement is traced against the background of American life, highlighting certain trends in the American Jewish community which were preconditions for the emergence of the movement. The role of the synagogue and the rabbi are extensively treated. The Conservative belief is clarified by demonstrating the various attitudes of the laity, the rabbinate and the "schoolmen." Schocken Books, 1972, $3.95.

————. *The Jew in American Society* and *The Jewish Community in America*. Two volumes offering the most recent examples of analytic writing about American Jewry by outstanding social scientists. Behrman House, 1974, $12.50 each.

—————————. *The Jews: Social Patterns of an American Group.* A collection of sociological studies of the American Jewish community and its institutions. Illinois Free Press, 1958, $10.95.

SLEEPER, JAMES A., and MINTZ, ALAN L., eds. *The New Jews.* New voices from the Jewish community discuss political radicalism, the State of Israel, the failure of suburban and campus Judaism, and the recovery of Jewish spirituality. Vintage, 1971, $2.45 paperback.

STROBER, GERALD S. *American Jews: Community in Crisis.* A survey of the current crisis confronting American Jews: Black anti-Semitism, "reverse quotas," Jews-for-Jesus movement, and the possible rift between Israel and the American Jewish community. Doubleday, 1974, $7.95.

TELLER, JUDD I. *Strangers and Natives.* The evolution of the American Jew from 1921 to 1967. Dell, 1970, $2.45 paperback.

UROFSKY, MELVIN I. *American Zionism from Herzl to the Holocaust.* A study of the Zionist movement in America and in American Jewish society from 1895 to the present. Doubleday, 1975, $12.50; 1976, $3.50 paperback.

WEISBORD, ROBERT G., and STEIN, ARTHUR. *Bittersweet Encounter: The Afro-American and the American Jew.* A history from the first encounters to the Black revolution, from mutual perceptions to the mutually destructive ideologies of perceived self-interest, anti-Semitism and white backlash. Schocken Books, 1972, $2.95.

WIERNIK, PETER, 3rd ed. *History of the Jews in America.* From the period of the discovery of America to the present. Hermon Press, 1973, $9.95.

JEWISH IDENTITY

ALLPORT, GORDON. *The Individual and His Religion.* A psychologist's assessment of religious modes of thought and experience and "the place of subjective religion in the structure of personality." Macmillan, 1962, $1.50 paperback.

BOROWITZ, EUGENE B. *The Mask Jews Wear: The Self-Deception of American Jewry.* Examines the rationale for Jewish existence and a philosophy of Jewishness that will hopefully result in adoption of a Jewish life-style. Simon & Schuster, 1973, $7.95.

BUBER, MARTIN, edited by Nahum Glatzer. *On Judaism.* Schocken, 1972, $2.95 paperback.

COHEN, HENRY, edited by Jack D. Spiro. *Why Judaism? A Search for Meaning in Jewish Identity.* Answers to fundamental questions. U.A.H.C., 1973, $3.00.

DE SOLA POOL, DAVID. *Why I Am a Jew.* Beacon Press, 1965, $1.25 paperback.

FLEG, EDMOND. *Why I Am a Jew.* Moving testimonial of a French intellectual who had turned his back on Judaism, felt lost, and returned. Bloch, 1975, $2.45.

FRIEDMAN, THEODORE. *Letters to Jewish College Students.* Questions about God, religion, and Jews and Judaism. Jonathan David, 1966, $1.95 paperback.

KAHANE, MEIR. *Never Again.* Victimized and persecuted throughout history, Jewish pride dictates that this must not happen again. Nash, 1972, $7.95.
Related titles: *Time to Go Home,* Nash, 1973, $7.95; *Our Challenge,* Chilton, 1974, $7.95; *The Story of the Jewish Defense League,* Chilton, 1975, $7.95.

LITVIN, BARUCH, and HOENIG, SIDNEY B., eds. *Jewish Identity: Modern Responsa and Opinions.* Leading scholars, religious thinkers, and jurists present their answers to the question, "Who is a Jew?" Feldheim, 1970, $9.75.

MEMMI, ALBERT. *Portrait of a Jew.* Translated by Elizabeth Abbott. Viking Press, 1962, $4.95, $2.95.

—————————. *The Liberation of the Jew.* Analyses of the Jewish psyche, Jewish thinking, the Jew as an individual and within society. Viking Compass, 1973, $2.95.

PATAI, RAPHAEL, and WING, JENNIFER P., eds. *The Myth of the Jewish Race.* A definition of race, the idea of "races" throughout history, and varying historical views of the Jews as a race. Scribner's, 1975, $14.95.

PORTER, JACK N., and DREIER, PETER, eds. *Jewish Radicalism: A Selected Anthology.* A compendium of the political voices and philosophies of the Jewish Liberation movement. Grove Press, 1973, $2.45 paperback.

PRAGER, DENNIS, and TELUSHKIN, JOSEPH. *Eight Questions People Ask About Judaism.* A lively, polemical response to questions on religion, ethics, Jewish nationhood and survival, Jewish-Christian relations, Marxism, etc. Tze Ulmad Press, 1975, $7.50.

RIESMAN, DAVID. *Individualism Reconsidered and Other Essays.* Free Press, 1954, $2.45 paperback. (See listing under *The Jew in America.*)

SCHACHTER, ZALMAN. *The First Step: A Primer of the Jew's Spiritual Life.* A Hasidic rabbi and mystic speaks to the existential concerns of young men and women. Published privately—available from the author, c/o University of Manitoba, Dept. of Religious Studies, Winnipeg.

SLEEPER, JAMES A., and MINTZ, ALAN L. *The New Jews.* New voices from the Jewish community discuss political radicalism, the State of Israel, the failures of suburban and campus Judaism, and the recovery of Jewish spirituality. Vintage/Random V-669, 1971, $2.45 paperback.

JEWISH LAW: HALACHAH

APPEL, GERSION. *A Philosophy of Mitzvot: The Religious-Ethical Concepts of Judaism, Their Roots in Biblical Law and the Oral Tradition.* This systematic treatment largely follows the medieval Sefer Ha-Hinukh, long recognized as a primary source for investigating the meaning and purpose of the Mitzvot. Ktav, 1975, $12.50; $4.95 paperback.

CHILL, ABRAHAM. *The Mitzvot.* The Mitzvot arranged according to the weekly readings of the Torah, explained from the classical commentaries. Bloch, 1974, $15.95.

COHEN, BOAZ. *Law and Tradition in Judaism.* Essays by one of the leading interpreters and exponents of the Conservative Movement. Ktav, 1959, $10.00.

DAVIDOVITCH, DAVID. *The Ketuba: Jewish Marriage Contracts Through the Ages.* Large, lavishly illustrated edition with text in Hebrew and English. E. Lewin-Epstein, Ltd., 1968, $24.95.

DONIN, HAYIM HALEVY. *To Be a Jew: A Guide to Jewish Observance in Contemporary Life.* (See listing under *Reference.*)

DORF, ELLIOT. *Jewish Law and Modern Ideology: A Confrontation Based on Source Materials.* United Synagogue, 1970, $5.75 paperback.

EPSTEIN, LOUIS M. *Marriage Laws in the Bible and the Talmud.* Johnson Repr., 1942, $12.50.

——————————. *Sex Laws and Customs in Judaism.* Ktav, 1968, $10.00.

FELDMAN, DAVID M. *Marital Relations, Birth Control and Abortion in Jewish Law.* (See listing under *Reference.*)

FREEHOF, SOLOMON. *Current Reform Responsa.* Ktav, 1969, $10.00.

GORDIS, ROBERT. *Sex and the Family in the Jewish Tradition.* Foreword by Marvin S. Weiner. The traditional code of Jewish morality is presented along with an analysis of the "new morality" and its likely consequences. United Synagogue, 1967, $1.25 paperback.

GRUNFELD, I. DAYAN. *The Jewish Dietary Laws.* Detailed, technical work. Soncino Press, 1972, $18.00, set.

HIRSCH, SAMSON RAPHAEL. *Horeb.* A classic of Jewish literature, it presents Jewish laws and observances in detail, with a comprehensive interpretation of their principles and philosophy. Soncino Press, 1962, $23.00, two-volume set.

JACOBOVITS, IMMANUEL. *Jewish Medical Ethics.* New, enlarged edition includes chapters on recent concerns such as abortion, homosexuality, euthanasia. Bloch, 1975, $5.95 paperback.

JACOBS, LOUIS. *Jewish Law.* Behrman House, 1968, $3.95.

KIRSCHENBAUM, AARON. *Self-Incrimination in Jewish Law.* Quite technical. The Burning Bush Press, 1970, $6.95.

LAMM, MAURICE. *The Jewish Way in Death and Mourning.* The laws and traditions are presented clearly. Jonathan David, 1969, $5.95 paperback.

LAMM, NORMAN. *A Hedge of Roses.* An explanation of the laws of family purity. Feldheim, 1966, $2.00.

ROSNER, FRED. *Studies in Torah Judaism: Modern Medicine and Jewish Law.* Abortion, euthanasia, artificial insemination, etc., from an Orthodox point of view. Bloch, 1972, $6.95 paperback.

SCHEINBERG, ABRAHAM. *What is Halachah?* A useful compendium of Jewish religious laws dealing with every aspect of Jewish life. Bloch, 1974, $15.00.

SILBERG, MOSHE. *Talmudic Law and the Modern State.* United Synagogue, 1973, $6.95.

SPERLING, ABRAHAM ISAAC. *Reason for Jewish Customs and Traditions.* Translated by Abraham Matts. The first English language edition of "Ta'amei Haminhagim" brings together Biblical, Talmudic, and Rabbinic explications. Bloch, 1968, $8.50.

JUDAISM AND CHRISTIANITY

BAECK, LEO. *Judaism and Christianity.* Translated and introduced by Walter Kaufmann. Five provocative essays on the historical relationships and differences between Judaism and Christianity. Atheneum, 1970, $2.95 paperback.

BISHOP, CLAIRE HUCHET. *How Catholics Look at Jews.* Quotations from and analyses of modern French, Italian, and Spanish teaching materials clearly indicate the extent of ignorance, bigotry and prejudice still directed at Jews. Paulist Press, 1974, $4.50 paperback.

BOKSER, BEN ZION. *Judaism and the Christian Predicament.* A historical and critical study of the common origins as well as the non-negotiable differences between Judaism and Christianity. Knopf, 1967, $6.95.

BUBER, MARTIN. *Two Types of Faith: The Interpretation of Judaism and Christianity.* The differences between the faiths are identified and clarified. Harper & Row, 1961, $2.50 paperback.

CHALMERS, R. C., and IRVING, JOHN A., eds. *The Meaning of Life in Five Great Religions.* Judaism as presented by Emil Fackenheim. Westminster Press, 1966, $1.95 paperback.

COHEN, ARTHUR A. *The Myth of the Judaeo-Christian Tradition and Other Dissenting Essays.* The author contends that there is no common Judaeo-Christian tradition but that there is, in fact, a tradition of theological enmity. Harper & Row, 1970, $7.50; Schocken, 1971, $2.75 paperback.

COHN, HAIM. *The Trial and Death of Jesus.* A Justice of Israel's Supreme Court, writing as an expert on Jewish legal history, probes the texts in the light of information we possess about Jewish and Roman law, the political and religious situation in the country, and reasons the Evangelists may have had for coloring the account. Harper & Row, 1971, $12.50.

DAVIES, WILLIAM D. *Paul and Rabbinic Judaism: Some Rabbinic Elements in Pauline Theology.* Harper, 1967, $2.75.

ENSLIN, MORTON SCOTT. *Christian Beginnings.* A concise treatment of the Jewish and pagan roots of Christianity and its historical genesis. Harper, 1956, $2.75 paperback.

—————————. *The Literature of the Christian Movement.* Supplement to author's *Christian Beginnings.* Harper, $3.25 paperback. Out of print.

FISHMAN, SAMUEL Z., ed. *Jewish Students and the Jesus Movement: A Campus Perspective.* A series of essays providing analyses and possible counter-strategies. B'nai B'rith Hillel, $1.50 paperback.

GLOCK, CHARLES, and STARK, RODNEY. *Christian Beliefs and Anti-Semitism.* A sociological study conducted in contemporary America. Careful analysis and statistical apparatus. Harper & Row, 1969, $1.95 paperback.

ISAAC, JULES, and BISHOP, CLAIRE HUCHET, eds. *Jesus and Israel.* Holt Rinehart and Winston, 1971, $12.50.

JURJI, EDWARD J. *The Great Religions of the Modern World.* A group of essays on the chief religions of the world. The essay by Abraham A. Neuman emphasizes Judaism's mix of particularism and universalism. Princeton Univ. Press, 1946, $10.50.

KATZ, JACOB. *Exclusiveness and Tolerance: Studies in Jewish-Gentile Relations in Medieval and Modern Times.* A brief, stimulating challenge to the notion of the one-sided development of Christian anti-Semitism. Schocken, 1962, $2.45 paperback.

LITTELL, FRANKLIN H. *The Crucifixion of the Jews.* A Christian view of the Jews as the Chosen People and the significance of the Holocaust and Israel restored. Harper & Row, 1974, $6.95.

OPSAH, PAUL D., and TANNENBAUM, MARC H., eds. *Speaking of God Today: Jews and Lutherans in Conversation.* Fortress Press, 1974, $6.95.

PARKES, JAMES. *The Conflict of Church and Synagogue: A Study in the Origins of Anti-Semitism.* Account of the early days of Jewish-Christian encounter, forming the basis of medieval and modern theological anti-Semitism. Atheneum, 1969, $4.95 paperback.

——————————. *Judaism and Christianity.* First published in 1948, this book wrestles with the ancient problems of theological and popular anti-Semitism. University of Chicago, 1975 reprint, $8.00.

Religion's Role in Racial Crisis. Prominent Christians and Jews discuss religious attitudes toward race and the responsibilities of the religiously committed in the struggle for social justice. Anti-Defamation League, 1963. Out of print.

RUETHER, ROSEMARY. *Faith and Fratricide.* An exploration of the theological roots of anti-Semitism. Seabury/Crossroads, 1974, $8.95.

——————————, ed. *Religion and Sexism—Images of Women in the Jewish and Christian Traditions.* Essays examining the historical relationship of patriarchal religions to feminine imagery. Simon & Schuster, 1974, $3.95.

RUNES, DAGOBERT. *Let My People Live.* How the anti-Jewish passages in the New Testament were exploited by Church and Christendom to promote Jew-hatred and murder. Philosophical Library, 1975, $5.00.

SANDMEL, SAMUEL. *A Jewish Understanding of the New Testament.* Ktav, 1974, $7.50 paperback.

——————————. *Two Living Traditions: Essays on Religion and the Bible.* Wayne State Univ. Press, 1972, $16.95.

——————————. *We Jews and Jesus: A Jewish Approach to Jesus.* Oxford, 1973, $1.95 paperback.

——————————. *The Genius of Paul: A Study in History.* Schocken Books SB-254, 1970, $2.45 paperback.

SCHONFIELD, HUGH J. *The Jesus Party.* An examination of the origins of the anti-Jewish bias of the New Testament and the early church. Macmillan, 1974, $7.95.

SILVER, ABBA HILLEL. *Where Judaism Differed.* A comparison with major religions. Macmillan, 1956, $5.95 cloth; 1972, $1.95 paperback.

TAL, URIEL. *Christians and Jews in Germany.* Religion, politics, and ideology in the Second Reich, 1870-1914. Cornell University Press, 1975, $19.50.

TRACHTENBERG, JOSHUA. *The Devil and the Jews.* An examination of the demonology and other suprarational components of medieval Christian anti-Semitism. Jewish Publication Society, 1943. Out of print.

WEISS-ROSMARIN, TRUDE. *Judaism and Christianity: The Differences.* An incisive and insightful presentation argued from the standpoint that interfaith understanding must not obliterate the real differences between the two religions. Jonathan David, 1965, $2.25 paperback.

LANGUAGES

ALCALAY, REUBEN, ed. *Complete Hebrew-English, English-Hebrew Dictionary.* Two volumes, authoritative reference. Hartmore House, 1962, 1965, $19.95 each; Massada Ltd., 1963.

BEN-YEHUDA, EHUD, and WEINSTEIN, DAVID, eds. *Ben-Yehuda's Pocket English-Hebrew, Hebrew-English Dictionary.* A convenient dictionary of modern Hebrew with a summary of Hebrew grammar. Washington Square Press, 1961, 1974, $1.25.

Berlitz Hebrew for Travellers. Useful phrases to guide you shopping, eating out, sightseeing, relaxing; phonetic pronunciation. Macmillan, 1975, $1.50.

BIRNBAUM, PHILIP. *Fluent Hebrew.* A bi-lingual text featuring several types of Hebrew usage—classical, newspaper, colloquial. Translations diminish as proficiency is attained. Large and systematic grammar section. Hebrew Publ. Co., 1966, $5.50.

BLUMBERG, HARRY. *Modern Hebrew Grammar and Composition.* A text for the high school and college levels. Hebrew Publishing Company, 1959, $4.50.

BROWN, FRANCIS; DRIVER, S. R.; and BRIGGS, C. A. *Hebrew and English Lexicon of the Old Testament.* Based on the thesaurus and lexicon of William Gesenius as translated by Edward Robinson. Oxford University Press, 1959, $25.00.

CHOMSKY, WILLIAM. *Hebrew, the Eternal Language.* The story of the development of the Hebrew language within the history of the Jewish people. Jewish Publication Society, 1957, $3.95 paperback.

GREENBERG, MOSHE. *Introduction to Hebrew.* A beginning, college-level text, designed to enable the student to read Biblical Hebrew. Prentice-Hall, 1964, $9.50.

Hebrew Language—30 Series. Two teaching cassettes, phrase dictionary and study guide in a handy pocket-size, book-shaped album. T. Y. Croweel, $14.95.

HOROWITZ, EDWARD. *How the Hebrew Language Grew.* The development of Hebrew with fascinating chapters on verb and noun patterns, borrowing, and transformations. Ktav, 1967, $6.95.

MADINA, MANN Z. *Arabic-English Dictionary of the Modern Literary Language.* Pocket Books, 1973, $2.50.

ROSTEN, LEO. *The Joys of Yiddish.* A hilarious dictionary and much more. Pocket Books, 1968, $1.95.

SIVAN, REUBEN, and LEVENSON, EDWARD, eds. *The Bantam Hebrew and English Megiddo Dictionary.* An up-to-date, comprehensive English-Hebrew and Hebrew-English dictionary, including essentials of grammar of both languages. Bantam Books, 1975, $1.95.

WEINGREEN, JACOB. *A Practical Grammar for Classical Hebrew.* Oxford, 1959, $9.00.

WEINREICH, URIEL. *College Yiddish.* An introduction to the Yiddish language and to Jewish life and culture. Yivo Institute for Jewish Research, 1949, fifth edition, 1971, $7.50.

ALTER, ROBERT. *After the Tradition: Essays on Modern Jewish Writing.* Dutton, 1964, $5.95 cloth; 1971, $1.95 paperback.

——————. *Modern Hebrew Literature.* An analytical anthology of the writings of major Hebrew authors since the Enlightenment. Behrman House, 1975, $12.50 cloth; $4.95 paperback.

BIN GORION, EMANUEL, ed. *Memekor Israel: Classical Jewish Folktales.* A treasury of more than 1000 tales that have enchanted generations of listeners and readers in centuries past. Two volumes. Univ. of Indiana Press, 1975, $42.50.

FIELD, LESLIE and JOYCE, eds. *Bernard Malamud: A Collection of Critical Essays.* Prentice-Hall, Spectrum, S-TC-123, 1970, $7.50 cloth.

GINZBERG, LOUIS. *Legends of the Jews.* Seven volumes that rank as the most significant work on Jewish folklore. Jewish Publication Society, 1961, $40.00 the set. Also: *Legends of the Bible,* 1975, single-volume edition, $7.95.

——————. *On Jewish Law and Lore.* Articles written for the Jewish Encyclopedia in 1912 on Talmud, Halachah, folklore, Kabbalah. Jewish Publication Society, 1970, $2.95 paperback.

GLATZER, NAHUM N. *The Judaic Tradition.* Excerpts from classical and historical literature from post-Biblical times to the present. Beacon Press, 1969, $4.95 paperback.

——————, ed. *Hammer on the Rock: A Midrash Reader.* Selections from Talmud and Midrash. Schocken Books, 1962, $2.25 paperback.

——————, ed. *The Jewish Reader.* Excerpts of classical literature from the Talmud to the Hasidic masters. Schocken, 1961, $2.95 paperback.

GUTTMANN, ALLEN. *The Jewish Writer in America: Assimilation and the Crisis of Identity.* Considers the Jewish writer within the context of his marginality and double alienation from his own heritage and the mainstream of American society. Oxford Univ. Press, 1971, $7.95.

HALKIN, SIMON. *Modern Hebrew Literature: From the Enlightenment to the State of Israel: Trends and Values.* Schocken, 1970 reprint of 1950 edition, $2.25 paperback.

HARAP, LOUIS. *The Image of the Jew in American Literature.* A study of anti-Semitic stereotypes in early American literature. Jewish Publication Society, 1975, $10.00.

HERTZBERG, ARTHUR, ed. *Judaism.* An extensive selection of brief excerpts from classical Jewish writings, organized with introductions and interpretations. Braziller, 1962. Out of print. Washington Press, 1963, paperback. Out of print.

HOWE, IRVING, and GREENBERG, ELIEZER, eds. *Voices from the Yiddish.* An anthology of essays, memoirs, diaries, reflecting the life and culture of the Yiddish-speaking world of Europe and America. Schocken Books, 1972, $4.95 paperback.

KRAVITZ, NATHANIEL. *3000 Years of Hebrew Literature: From the Earliest Times Through the 20th Century.* Survey. Swallow Press, 1971, $10.00.

LEVIANT, CURT. *Masterpieces of Hebrew Literature: A Treasury of 2,000 Years of Jewish Creativity.* Covering the major periods from the Apocrypha to the 18th century. Ktav, 1969, $10.00.

LIPTZIN, SOLOMON C. *The Jew in American Literature.* Traces the images and self-images of the American Jew as reflected in belles-lettres from the Colonial Era to the present. Bloch, 1966, $5.50.

—————————. *A History of Yiddish Literature.* Descriptions and evaluations of both major and minor Yiddish writers. Jonathan David, 1972, $10.00.

—————————. *The Flowering of Yiddish Literature.* A scholarly historical survey. $2.98.

LITERATURE AND LITERARY CRITICISM

MADISON, CHARLES. *Yiddish Literature: Its Scope and Major Writers.* Critical comment, summaries of plots, and historical analysis of Yiddish literature from Mendele to Singer. Schocken, 1971, $4.50 paperback.

MALIN, IRVING, ed. *Contemporary American Jewish Literature.* The achievements of contemporary Jewish-American literature and of its writers are critically examined in this collection of essays. Indiana University Press, 1973, $7.95.

MILLGRAM, ABRAHAM E., ed. *Anthology of Medieval Hebrew Literature.* Abelard, 1961, $7.95.

MIRON, DAN. *A Traveller Disguised: The Rise of Modern Yiddish Fiction in the 19th Century.* Concentrates on the seminal figure of Mendele the Bookpeddler but ranges far afield. Schocken, 1973, $10.95.

NOY, DOV. *Folktales of Israel.* Translated by Gene Baharav. A sampling of seventy-one tales. University of Chicago Press, FW-8, 1963, $2.95.

RIBALOW, MENACHEM. *Flowering of Modern Hebrew Literature.* A scholarly historical survey. Twayne, 1959, $7.50.

SAMUEL, MAURICE. *Prince of the Ghetto.* A selection and retelling of the stories of I. L. Peretz, the great Yiddish folk writer of Eastern Europe. Schocken, 1973, $2.45 paperback.

——————. *The World of Sholom Aleichem.* The humor and pathos of Sholom Aleichem, interpreted by a contemporary literary artist. Knopf, 1943, $5.95; Random, 1973, $2.45 paperback.

SCHURER, EMIL. *Literature of the Jewish People in the Time of Jesus.* Analysis of the major books of a crucial period with an introduction by Nahum Glatzer. Schocken Books, 1972, $4.50.

SCHWARTZ, LEO W., ed. *The Menorah Treasury.* The best stories, essays, memoirs, and verse from the "Menorah Journal" in one large volume. Illustrated. Slipcase. Jewish Publication Society, 1964, $10.00.

—————————, ed. *The Jewish Caravan.* Great stories of twenty-five centuries. A classic anthology. A definitive collection of Jewish stories, tales, and legends with appeal for all ages. Schocken, 1976, revised and enlarged. $9.95 paperback.

WAXMAN, MEYER. *History of Jewish Literature.* Six volumes. A comprehensive history of Jewish literature in Hebrew, Yiddish, English and other languages. A. S. Barnes, 1930-1941, $50.00.

ZINBERG, ISRAEL. *A History of Jewish Literature.* Classical Yiddish work, translated into English, tracing Jewish literature from the 10th century in Spain to 19th century Russian Haskalah. Ktav, Volumes I-V $15.00, Volumes VI-IX $17.50.

MUSIC, ART, DANCE, PHOTOGRAPHY

BERK, FRED. *Ha-Rikud: The Jewish Dance.* An instruction manual and capsule history of Jewish dance from Biblical times to the contemporary scene in Israel and America. U.A.H.C., 1972, $3.00 paperback.

COOPERSMITH, HARRY, ed. *The Songs We Sing.* Sabbath, holiday, and Israeli songs and old favorites (in transliterated Hebrew) with piano accompaniment. United Synagogue of America, 1950, $10.00.

DAYAN, RUTH, and FEINBERG, WILLIE. *Crafts of Israel.* An overview of Israeli crafts, their tradition, development, charm and diversity. Illustrated. Macmillan, 1975, $14.95.

EISENSTEIN, JUDITH KAPLAN. *Heritage of Jewish Music: The Music of the Jewish People.* Over 100 selections of music with songs translated into English from Hebrew, Yiddish and Ladino. U.A.H.C., 1972, $15.00.

GARVIN, PHILIP. *A People Apart: Hasidim in America.* Text by Arthur Cohen. E. P. Dutton, 1970, $20.00.

GORDIS, ROBERT, and DAVIDOWITZ, MOSHE, eds. *Art in Judaism— Studies in the Jewish Artistic Experience.* A collection of articles dealing with the relationship of the visual arts to the Jewish historical experience. National Council on Art in Jewish Life and Judaism, 1975, $5.95.

GUTMANN, JOSEPH, ed. *Beauty in Holiness: Studies in Jewish Ceremonial Art and Customs.* Ktav, 1970, $20.00.

HOLDE, ARTHUR, and HESKES, IRENE, eds. *Jews in Music: From the Age of Enlightenment to the Mid-Twentieth Century.* A survey of the Jewish contribution to sacred and secular music. Bloch, 1975, $7.95.

HUBMANN, FRANZ. *The Jewish Family Album: The Life of a People in Photographs.* Scenes of the years 1850 to 1945, from stark ghettos to the opulence of late nineteenth-century Europe. Little, Brown, 1975, $24.95.

IDELSOHN, ABRAHAM Z. *Jewish Music in its Historical Development.* Reissue of classic analysis of the history and characteristics of Jewish music from its Semitic, Oriental beginnings through the centuries. Holt, Rinehart and Winston, $7.50; Schocken, 1967, $3.95 paperback.

KAMPF, AVRAM. *Contemporary Synagogue Art.* Developments in synagogue art in the U.S., 1945-1965. A survey; includes 275 black and white illustrations, bibliography, index and notes. U.A.H.C., 1966, $12.50.

——————————. *Jewish Ceremonial Art and Religious Observance.* The history and legends that give meaning to ceremonial art, the observances that call it into being. Abrams, $25.00.

KATZ, KARL, et al. *From the Beginning: Archaeology and Art in the Israel Museum.* Illustrations from the Israel Museum collection. Reynal (Morrow), 1968, $15.00.

KINEAD, EUGENE, and VISHNIAC, ROMAN. *Roman Vishniac: An Appreciation.* Vishniac's now-familiar photographs taken in Poland in 1938 and examples of his outstanding photomicrography. Grossman-Viking, $7.50 paperback.

LANDSBERGER, FRANZ. *A History of Jewish Art.* Illustrated. Kennikat, 1973 reprint of 1946 edition, $17.50.

LAPSON, DVORA. *Jewish Dances the Year Round.* The music, words, directions for teaching, and costume suggestions for dances based on Jewish folkways, festivals, Hasidism, ceremonial life, and Israel. Board of Jewish Education, $3.50.

LEVEEN, JACOB. *The Hebrew Bible in Art.* An investigation of the range and character of Jewish religious art. Sefer Hermon Press, 1974, $12.50.

LEYMARIE, JEAN. *Jerusalem Windows of Mark Chagall.* Braziller, 1967, $7.95.

Masada Song Festival Song Book. Sixty-eight songs in Hebrew with transliteration and some English explanations; music not included. Zionist Organization of America, 1973, $1.25 paperback.

NULMAN, MACY. *Concise Encyclopedia of Jewish Music.* Covers a wide range of subjects and categories; liturgy, folk, theatre, and composers. McGraw-Hill, 1975, $13.95.

RASKIN, SAUL. *Hagadah for Passover.* Illus. Hebrew and English. Bloch, 1969, 2nd edition, $12.50.

——————. *Pirke Aboth.* Etchings with text and English and Yiddish translation. Bloch, 1940, $12.50.

ROCKLAND, MAE SHAFTER. *The Work of Our Hands: Jewish Needlecraft for Today.* Projects in needlepoint, embroidery, applique, quilting and patchwork with directions for each medium. Articles for personal use or to form a part of the Jewish tradition and ritual in the home. Schocken, 1973, $10.00 cloth; 1975, $5.95 paperback.

ROTH, CECIL, and NARKISS, BEZALEL. *Hebrew Illuminated Manuscripts.* Collection of Haggadot, Mahzorim, Siddurim—illuminated pages from medieval texts. Leon Amiel, 1969, $19.95.

ROTH, CECIL. *Jewish Art: An Illustrated History.* This lavishly illustrated book surveys the whole spectrum of Jewish artistic creativity from the earliest beginnings in Canaan to the present day. Revised and updated. New York Graphic Society, 1971, $20.00.

ROTHMULLER, ARON M. *The Music of the Jews.* A brief survey. A. S. Barnes, 1960, $1.65 paperback.

RUBENS, ALFRED. *History of Jewish Costume.* Development, significance of tradition, and regional influences from 4000 B.C.E. to the present. Richly illustrated. Crown Publishers, 1973, $15.00.

RUBIN, REUVEN. *My Life, My Art.* Reproductions of his best works. Sabra Books, $25.00. Out of print.

RUBIN, RUTH, ed. *A Treasury of Jewish Folksong.* Piano settings, English transliterations and translations from Hebrew and Yiddish. Also songs from World War II and modern Israel. Schocken, 1950, $6.95 paperback.

—————————. *Voices of a People.* The story of Yiddish folksong. Extensive historical and analytical text accompanies the texts of some 500 songs. A. S. Barnes, $8.50.

SENDREY, ALFRED. *Music of the Jews in the Diaspora* (up to 1800). A contribution to the social and cultural history of the Jews. A. S. Barnes, 1971, $18.00.

SHAHN, BEN. *The Alphabet of Creation.* A legend from the Zohar turned into visual magic by the great graphic artist. Schocken Books, SF-3, 1965, $2.25.

SHARON, RUTH. *Arts and Crafts the Year Round.* Two illustrated volumes, including projects related to every aspect of Jewish life. United Synagogue, 1965, $25.00.

SHECHORI, RAN; ZAPHIR, ISRAEL, Photographer. *Art in Israel.* Contemporary Israeli painters and sculptors, their lives and work. Sadan, 1974, $10.00.

SHULMAN, AVRAHAM. *The Old Country.* Foreword by Isaac Bashevis Singer. A book of photographs showing the world from which the ancestors of most American Jews migrated. Scribner's, 1975, $12.50; $7.95 paperback.

TAMUZ, BENJAMIN, ed. *Art in Israel.* Translated from Hebrew. Survey of the development of art in Israel since the turn of the century. International Publishing Service, 1966, $25.00.

VISHNIAC, ROMAN. *Polish Jews. A Pictorial Record.* Foreword by Abraham Joshua Heschel. Memorable photos of unforgettable faces. Schocken, 1947, $2.95.

WIGODER, GEOFFREY. *Jewish Art and Civilization.* Studies written by outstanding scholars. Profusely illustrated. Walker, two volumes, $75.00.

POETRY

AMICHAI, YEHUDA. Trans. by Harold Schimmel. *Songs of Jerusalem and Myself*. A collection of poems for which the translator received the Jewish Book Council's Kovner Award for Poetry, 1974. Harper & Row, 1973, $2.95 paperback.

AUSUBEL, NATHAN and MARYANN, eds. *A Treasury of Jewish Poetry*. Familiar anthology. Crown, 1957, $6.95.

BIALIK, HAYYIM NACHMAN. Trans. by Israel Efros. *Selected Poems: Hayyim Nachman Bialik*. Block, 1965, $5.50.

——————————. *Selected Poems*. Translated by Maurice Samuel. Illustrated by Maida Silverman. Some of the best-known poems. UAHC, 1972, $12.50.

BIRMAN, ABRAHAM. *An Anthology of Hebrew Poetry*. A long introductory essay on the development of Hebrew poets and poetry. Abelard Schuman, 1968, $7.95.

BURNSHAW, STANLEY; CARMI, T.; and SPICEHANDLER, EZRA, eds. *The Modern Hebrew Poem Itself: From the Beginnings to the Present: 69 Poems*. Examples, interpretations, and explications. Schocken, 1966, $5.95 paperback.

COHEN, JOSEPH. *Journey to the Trenches: The Life of Isaac Rosenberg, 1890-1918*. The first complete biography of the great English war poet who grew up in London's East End, the son of impoverished Russian immigrant parents. Basic Books, 1975, $12.50.

GLATSTEIN, JACOB. *Selected Poems*. The poetry of one of the great modern Yiddish writers and poets, sensitively translated by Ruth Whitman. October House, 1973, $2.95 paperback.

GOLDSTEIN, DAVID, translator. *The Jewish Poets of Spain*. Anthology of poetry from the Goldern Age of Spanish Jewry. Penguin Books, L-250, 1972, $1.95.

HALEVI, JEHUDAH. *Selected Poems*. Trans. by Nina Salaman. By the great philosopher and poet of the Spanish Golden Age. Jewish Publication Society, $3.95.

HOWE, IRVING, and GREENBERG, ELIEZER, eds. *A Treasury of Yiddish Poetry*. Anthology of major Yiddish poets of 19th and 20th century. Holt, Rinehart and Winston, 1969, $4.95; Schocken, 1976, $5.95 paperback.

IBN GABIROL, SOLOMON. *Selected Religious Poems.* Trans. by Israel Zangwill and edited by Israel Davidson. By the famous poet and philosopher of the Golden Age in Spain. Bi-Lingual, Jewish Publication Society, 1974, $3.95.

JAFFE, MARIE B. *Ten For Posterity: An Anthology of Yiddish Poems.* The poems cover a broad spectrum from folklore to expressions of spirituality and mysticism. Compiled and translated by the author of "Gut Yuntif, Gut Yohr." Exposition Press, 1972, $5.00.

KLEIN, A.M. *The Collected Poems of A. M. Klein.* Compiled and with an introduction by Miriam Waddington. The complete verse of the Canadian Jewish poet. McGraw-Hill, 1974, $5.95 paperback.

KOLMAR, GERTRUDE. *Dark Soliloquy; The Selected Poems of Gertrude Kolmar.* Foreword by Cynthia Ozick. The work of the great German poet, who died in Auschwitz in 1943. Seabury Press, 1975, $8.95.

KOVNER, ABBA. *A Canopy in the Desert.* Translated by Shirley Kaufman. Selected poems by one of Israel's finest poets. Pittsburgh Univ. Press, 1973, $3.95 paperback.

LEFTWICH, JOSEPH. *The Golden Peacock: A Worldwide Treasury of Yiddish Poetry.* Out of print, but still the finest collection of Yiddish poetry in English translation. Thomas Yoseloff.

MINTZ, RUTH F. *Modern Hebrew Poetry: A Bilingual Anthology.* One hundred and fifteen poems represent the styles and themes of twenty-eight important poets of the century. Voweled Hebrew original pages face the English translations. Univ. of California Press, 1966, $3.50.

POETRY

SACHS, NELLY. *O the Chimneys.* Translated from the German by Michael Hamberger et al. Selected poems including "Eli," a verse play, by the winner of the Nobel Prize for Literature, 1966. Farrar, Straus & Giroux, 1967, $7.50 cloth; $2.75 paperback.

SHAPIRO, KARL. *Poems of a Jew.* Poems reflecting the poet's obsession with his people. Random House, 1958, $5.95.

WHITMAN, RUTH, ed. *An Anthology of Modern Yiddish Poetry.* The original poems in Yiddish with English translations. October House, 1966, $2.95 paperback.

ZELDIS, CHAIM. *May My Words Feed Others.* An anthology of verse and fiction from the *Reconstructionist* magazine. A. S. Barnes, 1973, $12.95.

PRAYER

(See also: Sabbath, Festivals and Practices)

ABRAHAMS, ISRAEL. *A Companion to the Authorized Daily Prayer Book.* A page-by-page commentary to the siddur, with notes, history, and sources of the prayers and services. Sepher Hermon Press, 1966, $4.75.

AGNON, S. Y. *Days of Awe.* An anthology of legends and traditions for Rosh Hashanah and Yom Kippur. Schocken, 1965, $7.50 cloth; $2.95 paperback.

ARZT, MAX. *Justice and Mercy.* A detailed commentary on the liturgy of the New Year and Day of Atonement. Holt, Rinehart and Winston, 1963, $4.95.

BAUMGARD, HERBERT M. *Judaism and Prayer.* An introductory text on "Growing toward God." U.A.H.C., 1964, $1.50.

BEMPORAD, JACK, ed. *A Reform Jewish Perspective.* Papers on diverse traditionalist, existentialist, naturalist and organicist views. U.A.H.C., 1967, $2.25 paperback.

CASPER, BERNARD M. *Talks on Jewish Prayer.* A general introduction to the language and structure of prayer and the worship services. World Zionist Organization, Department for Torah Education, 1963, $1.30.

DEROVAN, DAVID J. *Prayer.* A first-rate anthology and study guide to the philosophy and meaning of Tefilla. Yavneh Studies # 3, 1970, $2.00.

DE SOLA POOL, DAVID. *The Kaddish.* A scholarly study of the hallowed and memorable prayer. Union of Sephardic Congregations, 1964.

DRESNER, SAMUEL H. *Prayer, Humility, and Compassion.* A small anthology of psalm and parable, examples of Jewish saintliness, and aspects of Jewish experience. Prayerbook Press, 1957, $3.95 cloth.

GARFIEL, EVELYN. *The Service of the Heart.* The development of the traditional Siddur and the significance of its prayers. A. S. Barnes, 1958, $5.95 cloth; Wilshire Book Co., $3.00 paperback.

GLATZER, NAHUM, N., editor. *The Language of Faith*. A selection from the most expressive Jewish prayers. Schocken, 1967, $4.95.

GOLDSTEIN, ROSE. *A Time to Pray: A Personal Approach to the Jewish Prayerbook*. Combines historical facts, personal anecdotes, spiritual guidance, and philosophical wisdom. Women's League for Conservative Judaism, 1972, $6.95.

GREEN, ALLAN S. *Return to Prayer: Home and Student Devotions for Sabbath, Every Day and Special Occasions*. U.A.H.C., 1971.

GREENBERG, SIDNEY, and SUGARMAN, S. ALLAN. *Contemporary High Holiday Service for Teenagers and . . .* A modern service incorporating (in addition to Hebrew prayers) writings, interpretations, photographs, and illustrations. Loose-leaf format. Prayer Book Press, 1970, $3.95.

GREENBERG, SIDNEY, translator and compiler. *Likrat Shabbat*. Combines traditional Hebrew liturgy and song with new prayers, explanatory notes, and an extensive selection of contemporary materials for worship, study and song. Media Judaica, Hartmore House, 1973, $7.95, includes cassette.

HERTZ, JOSEPH H. *Authorized Daily Prayer Book*. English and Hebrew. Richly annotated. Bloch, 1961, $12.50.

HESCHEL, ABRAHAM JOSHUA. *Man's Quest for God*. Studies in prayer and symbolism deal with the way, the goal and the approach to a life of religious insight and the attempt to regain the sense of mystery that animates all beings. Scribner's, 1954, $5.95.

HEINEMAN, JOSEPH, and PETUCHOWSKI, JAKOB. *The Literature of the Synagogue*. A three-part introduction to the textual heritage of Jewish devotion: (1) selections of prayers and liturgies; (2) sermons from the Rabbinic period; (3) sacred poems and devotional hymns. Behrman House, 1975, $12.50.

IDELSOHN, ABRAHAM Z. *Jewish Liturgy In Its Historical Development.* Schocken, 1967, $3.95 paperback.

JACOBS, LOUIS. *Hasidic Prayer.* A systematic study of the methods of prayer of the Hasidic community. Schocken, 1973, $10.00.

JACOBSON, B. S. *Meditations on the Siddur.* Translated by Rabbi Leonard Oschry. Studies in the essential problems and ideas of Jewish worship, and the halachic and philosophic problems in prayer. Sinai Publishing Co, Tel Aviv, 1966, $6.50.

——————. *The Weekday Siddur.* An exposition and analysis of its structure, contents, language, and ideas. Sinai Publishing Co., Tel Aviv, 1973, $10.00.

KADUSHIN, MAX. *Worship and Ethics: A Study in Rabbinic Judaism.* (See listing under *Rabbinic Judaism.*)

KIEVAL, HERMAN. *The High Holidays: A Commentary on the Prayerbook of Rosh Hashanah and Yom Kippur.* Discusses the origin and development of the services and individual prayers. Includes a glossary of Hebrew words and phrases. Burning Bush Press, 1959, $5.00.

KON, ABRAHAM. *Prayer.* The history and development of the worship service and the synagogue, including sections on the meaning and the act of prayer and ritual. Soncino Press, 1971, $6.50.

Magill's Complete Linear Prayerbook with Services for the Sabbath and the Festivals. The traditional prayerbook presented in short facing columns of Hebrew and English. One of the best ways to study prayer, whether for content or language. Hebrew Publ. Co., 1905, $4.00 (frequently reprinted).

MARTIN, BERNARD. *Prayer in Judaism.* New translations of some fifty of the most important prayers from the whole range of Jewish devotional literature. Each prayer acompanied by interpretive commentary. Basic Books, 1968, $7.50.

MILLGRAM, ABRAHAM E. *Jewish Worship.* The *siddur* as a living, growing organism reflecting the deepest Jewish commitments to ideas and ideals about God, the good life, and the hope for an ideal society. Jewish Publication Society, 1971, $8.50.

PETUCHOWSKI, JAKOB, ed. *Understanding Jewish Prayer*. A significant statement by a Reform rabbi. Ktav, 1972, $8.95.

ROSSEL, SEYMOUR. Edited by Eugene B. Borowitz and Hyman Chanover. *When a Jew Prays*. A religious school text. Excellent presentation makes this useful in teaching on a beginner's level at any age. Behrman House, 1974, $4.75.

STITSKIN, LEON D., editor. *Studies in Torah Judaism*. Contains two major monographs, "The Kaddish: Man's Reply to the Problem of Evil" by Martin Luban, and "Prayers" by Eliezer Berkovits. Ktav, 1969, $15.00.

ADLER, MORRIS. *The World of the Talmud.* A short study which, though centered on the Talmud and its teachings, reveals much about the historical development and essential character of Judaism. Schocken, 1963, $1.75 paperback.

BARON, SALO W., and BLAU, JOSEPH L., eds. *Judaism: Post-Biblical and Talmudic Period.* A collection of source materials. Bobbs Merrill, 1954, $6.50.

BELKIN, SAMUEL. *In His Image: The Jewish Philosophy of Man as Expressed in the Rabbinic Tradition.* Abelard Schuman, 1960, $6.50.

BIRNBAUM, PHILIP, ed. *Mishnah Torah of Moses Maimonides.* An abridged translation of Maimonides' comprehensive codification of Jewish law. Hebrew Publ. Co., 1975, $3.95 paperback (English).

BOROWITZ, EUGENE B. *Choosing a Sex Ethic: A Jewish Inquiry.* A sympathetic and insightful clarification of the compelling sexual and moral issues facing young adults today. Schocken, 1970, $2.45 paperback.

COHEN, ABRAHAM. *Everyman's Talmud.* A concise summary of Talmudic teachings about religion, jurisprudence, folklore and ethics. Dutton, 1949, $7.95; Schocken, 1975, $6.95.

DANBY, HERBERT, trans. *The Mishna.* (See listing under *Classics in Translation.*)

DAUBE, DAVID. *Collaboration with Tyranny in Rabbinic Law.* Oxford Univ. Press, 1965, $3.25.

The El-Am Talmud. A new edition of the Talmud, appearing in monthly installments and intended for the beginning student. Each page contains the vocalized Aramaic text, plus English translation, summary and highly illuminating commentaries. Issues to date are: Berakhot, Kiddushin, and Bava Metzeiah. National Academy for Adult Jewish Studies. Annual subscription, $19.00—ten 16-page booklets.

FINKELSTEIN, LOUIS. *Akiba: Scholar, Saint and Martyr.* A pleasant retelling of many of the Aggadot of Rabbinic lore about the great
teachers from Hillel to Akiba. Atheneum, 1970, $3.25 paperback.

FREEHOF, SOLOMON B. *The Responsa Literature* and *A Treasury of
Responsa.* An introduction to the nature of this most important genre
of Rabbinic writing. Ktav, 1963, $15.00, two volumes in one.

GINZBERG, LOUIS. *On Jewish Law and Lore.* Essays on the development
of Halachah and Aggadah, the Talmud, and Kabbalah. Jewish
Publication Society, 1970, $2.95 paperback.

GLATZER, NAHUM, N., ed. *Hammer on the Rock: A Midrash Reader.* An
introduction to the literature of the Midrash, which has trans-
formed the words of the Bible into vehicles for religious insights.
Schocken, 1962, $2.25 paperback.

——————————. *Hillel the Elder: The Emergence of Classical Judaism.* A charm-
ing monograph; the rest is commentary. Schocken, 1966, $1.75
paperback. Out of print.

GOLDIN, JUDAH. *The Fathers According to Rabbi Nathan.* Schocken, 1955,
$4.95 paperback.

——————————. *The Living Talmud: A Commentary on Pirke Abot.* A good
introduction to the study of the Talmud. New American Library,
1957, $1.25 paperback.

GORDIS, ROBERT. *Sex and the Family in the Jewish Tradition.* An authoritative, yet popular, treatment of areas of fundamental importance.
Burning Bush Press, 1967, $1.25 paperback.

HERFORD, R. TRAVERS, ed. *The Ethics of the Talmud: Sayings of the Fathers.*
The complete Hebrew text of the famous collection of maxims
from the Mishnah, with English translation and commentary.
Schocken, 1962, $3.50 cloth; $1.95 paperback.

——————————. *Talmud and Apocrypha.* Reprint of 1929 edition. Ktav,
$10.00.

HERTZ, JOSEPH H. *The Midrash Rabbah.* Ten volumes. Soncino, $165.00 the set.

KADUSHIN, MAX. *The Rabbinic Mind.* An investigation into the categories of Rabbinic thinking. Bloch, 1972, $9.75; $4.95 paperback.

—————————. *Worship and Ethics: A Study in Rabbinic Judaism.* A treatment of these two aspects of classical Judaism provides some valuable insights into the character of Rabbinic thought and Jewish liturgy. Northwestern University Press, 1964, $10.50; Bloch, 1974, $5.95 paperback.

KIRSCHENBAUM, AARON. *The Talmud and You.* Discussion of "The Jewish Wedding Ceremony," "How to Quarrel Constructively— the Talmudic Concept and Practice," "Love Thy Neighbor—The Letter and Spirit in Jewish Law," "Crime and Punishment—An Introduction to Rabbinic Legal Theory." Highly recommended. Hadassah Education Dept.

LAUTERBACH, JACOB Z. *Rabbinic Essays.* (Hebrew Union College Press) Ktav, 1950, $17.50.

LEHRMAN, S. M. *The World of the Midrash.* A popular interpretation of Rabbinic theology citing basic concepts. Yoseloff, 1962, $2.95 cloth; $1.45 paperback. Out of print.

LIPMAN, EUGENE J., ed. *The Mishnah: Oral Teachings of Judaism.* Selected materials, newly translated, with short commentaries. Norton, 1970, $6.95; Schocken, 1974, $3.95 paperback.

LUZZATO, MOSES HAYYIM. *Mesillat Yesharim: The Path of the Upright.* (See listing under *Classics in Translation.*)

MEILZINER, MOSES. *Introduction to the Talmud.* Fourth edition, Bloch, 1967, $7.50.

MONTEFIORE, CLAUDE JOSEPH, and LOEWE, HERBERT, eds. *A Rabbinic Anthology.* Foreword by Raphael Loewe. A vast compendium of passages, parables and statements of Talmudic and Midrashic literature. Schocken, 1974, $20.00 cloth; $7.50 paperback.

MOORE, GEORGE FOOTE. *Judaism in the First Centuries of the Christian Era: The Age of the Tanaim.* An excellent introduction to the significant religious issues of the rabbinic period. Schocken Books, 1971, two volumes, $8.50 and $7.50 paperback.

NEUSNER, JACOB. *Invitation to the Talmud: A Teaching Book.* An introduction to the Talmud and its importance for modern man. Harper & Row, 1974, $4.95 paperback.

——————. *From Politics to Piety: The Emergence of Pharasaic Judaism.* Selections from Josephus, the Gospels and the Talmud. Prentice-Hall, 1973, $3.95 paperback.

——————. *History and Torah: Essays On Jewish Learning.* The acquisition of the Jewish heritage through study, the special problems and values inherent in such study for the modern Jew and the lives of past great exemplars of Jewish learning. Schocken Books, 1965, $1.95 paperback.

SCHECHTER, SOLOMON. *Aspects of Rabbinic Theology: Major Concepts of the Talmud.* With an introduction by Louis Finkelstein. The classic statement of those ideas that form the religious consciousness of the Jewish people. Schocken, 1961, $3.95.

SILVERMAN, WILLIAM. *Rabbinic Wisdom and Jewish Values.* A selection from the Midrash. U.A.H.C., 1971, $2.50 paperback.

STRACK, HERMANN L. *Introduction to the Talmud and Midrash.* A guide to Rabbinic literature includes the history, contents and principal figures of the Mishnah, the Talmuds of Palestine and Babylonia, the Tosefta, and the Midrashim. Atheneum, 1969, $3.95 paperback.

REFERENCE

AHARONI, YOHANAN, and AVI-YONAH, MICHAEL. *The Macmillan Bible Atlas.* All the periods and important events of Jewish history depicted in detail; includes 262 large territorial maps, a key to the maps, and a chronology of early civilizations. Macmillan, 1968, $9.95.

ALCALAY, REUBEN. *Basic Encyclopedia of Jewish Proverbs, Quotations and Folk Wisdom.* A valuable, varied anthology arranged alphabetically by subject. Hartmore House, 1975, $18.95.

The American Jewish Yearbook. Articles on significant developments in the Jewish world each year, with statistics and information on Jewish organizational and communal life throughout the world. American Jewish Committee and Jewish Publication Society, Vol. 74, 1974, $13.50.

BAHAT, DAN. *Jerusalem Atlas.* Tracing the history of Jerusalem from ancient times to the present. Scribner's, 1975, $5.95.

BARON, JOSEPH, ed. *Treasury of Jewish Quotations.* A. S. Barnes, 1965, $10.00.

BIRNBAUM, PHILIP. *A Book of Jewish Concepts.* A handy one-volume reference work for use of the modern English-speaking reader. Hebrew Publ. Co., 1975, $7.50.

BROWN, FRANCIS; DRIVER, S. R.; and BRIGGS, C. A. *Hebrew and English Lexicon of the Old Testament.* Based on the thesaurus and lexicon of William Gesenius. Oxford University Press, 1959, $25.00.

COHEN, HARRY A., ed. *A Basic Jewish Encyclopedia.* Foreword by Dr. Louis Finkelstein. Includes the most important Jewish principles and practices, categorized according to Orthodox, Conservative and Reform observances. Hartmore House, 1965, $4.95.

COMAY, JOAN. *Who's Who in Jewish History After the Period of the Old Testament.* David McKay, 1974, $16.95.

DONIN, HAYYIM HALEVY. *To Be A Jew: A Guide to Jewish Observance in*

Contemporary Life. A practical reference guide to the laws and customs of Judaism as they apply to daily life in the contemporary world— chapters on ethics, Torah, commandments, dietary laws, family life, charity and community, and observances for all occasions of the holy day and family cycles. Basic Books, 1972, $10.95.

DUBNOW, SIMON. *History of the Jews.* Translated by Moshe Spiegel. One of the leading 19th-century scholars offers his interpretation. A. S. Barnes, 5 vols., 1968-1973, $10.00 each.

Encyclopedia Judaica. A comprehensive reference book, with contributions by leading Jewish scholars. Keter, 1972, 16 volumes, $615.00.

FELDMAN, DAVID M. *Marital Relations, Birth Control, and Abortion in Jewish Law.* A comprehensive treatment of the Rabbinic and later legal traditions that underlie Jewish values with respect to marriage, sex, and procreation, with comparative reference to the Christian tradition. Schocken, 1974, $3.95 paperback.

FREEDMAN, WARREN. *The Selected Guide for the Jewish Traveler.* A world guide to restaurants (also kosher), hotels, communal and cultural organizations, landmarks, scenery, synagogues, rabbis, and phone numbers of hospitable Jewish residents. Macmillan, 1972, $2.95.

GILBERT, MARTIN. *Atlas of the Arab-Israeli Conflict.* A visual narrative in 101 maps. Macmillan, 1975, $6.95.

—————————. *Jewish History Atlas.* 112 maps from Biblical times to the present. Macmillan, 1969, $4.95.

Hebrew-English Lexicon of the Bible. Schocken Books, 1975, $2.95.

HIMMELFARB, MILTON, and FEIN, LEONARD, eds. *American Jewish Yearbook.* Latest edition of popular annual reference work of trends in American and Jewish life. Jewish Publication Society, $13.50, Vol. 74.

The Interpreter's Dictionary of the Bible. A scholarly encyclopedia explaining concepts, personalities and events, and including an historical atlas.

Abingdon Press, 1962, $45.00, 4 volumes.

ISAACSON, BEN, and WIGODER, DEBORAH. *The International Jewish Encyclopedia*. Lavishly illustrated. Prentice-Hall, 1973, $10.95.

JASTROW, MARCUS. *A Dictionary of the Targumim, Talmud, and Midrash*. Classic one-volume Aramaic dictionary. Judaica, 1971, $15.00.

The Jewish Book Annual. Edited by A. Alan Steinbach. Bibliographies and articles. Jewish Book Council, Vol. 33, 1975-76, $8.00.

The Jewish Encyclopedia. The standard reference work in English for information relating to Jewish history, religion, literature, including many classic articles and abundant illustrations. A reprint of the classic 1905 edition. Ktav, 1964, $150, 12 volumes.

POSTAL, BERNARD, and KOPPMAN, LIONEL. *A Jewish Tourist's Guide to the U.S.* Jewish Publication Society, 1954, $5.00. Out of print. Also: *Jewish Landmarks in New York*. An informal history and guide. Hill and Wang, 1964, $2.45.

ROSEN, DOV. *Shema Yisrael*. Zion Tallis Book Division, 1972, $12.95, 2 vols.

ROTH, CECIL, ed. *The New Standard Jewish Encyclopdia*. Doubleday, 1966, $19.95.

SPALDING, HENRY D. *Encyclopedia of Jewish Humor from Biblical Times to the Modern Age*. Jonathan David, rev. ed. 1973, $7.95.

SPIER, ARTHUR. *The Comprehensive Hebrew Calendar*. Structure and history of the Hebrew calendar and 100 years of corresponding dates. Behrman House, 1952, $9.00.

Universal Jewish Encyclopedia and Reader's Guide. Ten volumes and reader's guides. Ktav, 1944, $150.00 (700 pages).

VILNAY, ZEV. *The New Israel Atlas: Bible to Present Day*. 112 pages, 190 photographs, maps and drawings. McGraw-Hill, 1968, $7.95.

REFERENCE

WERBLOWSKY, RAPHAEL, and WIGODER, GEOFFREY, eds. *Encyclopedia of the Jewish Religion*. Holt, Rinehart and Winston, 1966, $18.00.

WIGODER, GEOFFREY, ed. *Everyman's Judaica*. Basic facts on outstanding persons, places, events in Jewish history and culture at a glance. Leon Amiel, 1975, $30.00.

BARON, SALO W. *The Russian Jews Under Tsars and Soviets.* A history of Jewish interaction with Russian governments and people. Macmillan, 1975, $12.95.

BEN AMI (pseud.). *Between Hammer and Sickle.* Informative description of the plight of Soviet Jewry in historical context. Jewish Publication Society, 1968, $6.00.

BILLINGTON, JAMES H. *The Icon and the Ax: An Interpretive History of Russian Culture.* While not primarily concerned with Jewish-Russian interaction, the book considers Jewish influences upon Russian Orthodoxy. Random House, Vintage, V-620, 1970, $3.95 paperback.

CHESLER, EVAN. *The Russian Jewry Reader.* A brief history of Russian Jewry and an analysis of their present plight. Behrman House, 1975, $2.45 paperback.

COHEN, RICHARD, ed. *Let My People Go.* Anthology of documents, articles, speeches, eye witness reports of the battle for freedom. Popular Library, 1975, $1.25 paperback.

DUBNOW, SIMON. *A History of the Jews in Russia and Poland.* A reprint of a classic. 3 volumes, Arno, reprint of 1920 edition, $60.00; Ktav, revised ed., 1973, $35.00.

ECKMAN, LESTER. *Soviet Policy Towards Jews and Israel, 1917-1974.* A survey. Shengold, 1975, $6.95.

FRUMKIN, JACOB, ed. *Russian Jewry, 1860-1917.* A. S. Barnes, 1965, $12.00.

——————————. *Russian Jewry, 1917-1967.* Translated by Joel Carmichael. A. S. Barnes, 1969, $12.00.

GILBOA, YEHOSHUA A. *The Black Years of Soviet Jewry.* The Stalin years, 1933-1953. Little, Brown, 1971, $15.00.

ISRAEL, GERALD. *The Jews in Russia.* Translated by Sanford Chernoff.

A documented history tracing official government prejudice all the way back to the era of Catherine the Great. St. Martin's Press, 1974, $10.00.

KOCHAN, LIONEL, ed. *Jews in Soviet Russia Since 1917.* (2nd edition) Oxford Univ. Press, 1973, $12.50.

KOREY, WILLIAM. *The Russian Cage: Antisemitism in Russia.* From Babi Yar to the Leningrad Trials, the multifaceted character of Soviet anti-Semitism, and its moral and legal issues. Viking Press, 1974, $12.95.

Letters from the Prisoners of Zion. English translations of letters from Jewish prisoners of conscience, smuggled out of prison camps. SSSJ, 1975, $2.00. SSSJ has a variety of pamphlets and programmatic material available. Write to Student Struggle for Soviet Jewry, 200 W. 72nd St., New York, N.Y. 10023.

MANDELSTAM, NADEZHDA. *Hope Abandoned.* Trans. by Max Hayward. A personal memoir by the widow of the poet Osip Mandelstam. Atheneum, 1974, $12.95.

NEDAVA, JOSEPH. *Trotsky and the Jews.* Trotsky's life and career viewed against his Jewish background. His conflicts and ambivalences, his attitude toward Zionism and the extent to which anti-Semitism was involved in his power struggle with Stalin. Jewish Publication Society, 1972, $6.00.

PORATH, JONATHAN D. *Jews in Russia: Last Four Centuries.* A popular survey of the main currents of Jewish life in Russia. United Synagogue, 1973, $2.95 paperback.

PULEREVITCH, YECHEZKEL. *Short Stories of the Long Death.* The author spent 17 years in Soviet prison camps. The stories communicate the desolation of the landscape, the inhumanities of the prison system, but also the invincibility of the human spirit. Student Struggle for Soviet Jewry, 1975, $6.95.

RUSINEK, ALLA. *Like a Song, Like a Dream.* The true story of a Soviet Jewish girl who reached freedom and a new life in Israel. Jewish Publication Society, 1973, $7.95.

SCHECHTMAN, JOSEPH B. *Star in Eclipse: Russian Jewry Revisited.* Report on Soviet Jewish cultural life. Yoseloff, 1961. Out of print.

SCHROETER, LEONARD. *The Last Exodus.* The growth and progress of the Jewish liberation movements in the Soviet Union, particularly since the Six-Day War, with the historical background and important new information. Universe Books, 1974, $10.95.

SOLOMON, MICHAEL. *Magadan.* The story of the author's eight years of imprisonment in Siberian camps. Auerbach Publishers, 1971, $8.95.

SOLZHENITSYN, ALEXANDER I. *Gulag Archipelago.* 2 volumes, Harper & Row, 1975, $1.95 each volume, paperback.

TELLER, JUDD I. *The Kremlin, the Jews and the Middle East.* Yoseloff, 1957, out of print.

WIESEL, ELIE. *Zalmen, or the Madness of God.* A play about the plight of Soviet Jewry struggling to survive, yet longing for something more than survival. Random House, 1975, $6.95.

——————. *The Jews of Silence.* Wiesel's trip to the Soviet Union. Holt, Rinehart, and Winston, 1966 $4.95; N.A.L., 1972, $1.95 paperback.

AGNON, S. Y. *Days of Awe.* Introduction by Judah Goldin. A treasury of traditions, legends, and learned commentaries concerning Rosh Hashanah, Yom Kippur, and the days between, by one of the greatest modern Hebrew writers. Schocken, 1965, $3.45 paperback.

ARZT, MAX. *Justice and Mercy.* (See listing under *Prayer.*)

BIRNBAUM, PHILIP, ed. *Daily Prayer Book: HaSiddur HaShalem.* The traditional liturgy for weekdays, Sabbaths, festivals and special occasions, with a parallel English translation and brief explanatory notes. Hebrew Publishing Co., 1949, $8.50, leather; $5.50 cloth.

BRAUDE, WILLIAM G., and KAPSTEIN, ISRAEL J., eds. *Pesikta de Rab Kahana.* A classic compilation of discourses for special Sabbaths and Festivals delivered in the Palestinian synagogue. Jewish Publication Society, 1975, $15.00.

DEROVAN, DAVID J., and BERLINER, MOSHE. *The Passover Haggadah.* A large-print Haggadah with traditional commentary and a comprehensive selection of Passover Halachot. Student Organization of Yeshiva Univ., $2.50.

DONIN, HAYIM HALEVY. *To Be A Jew: A Guide to Jewish Observance in Contemporary Life.* (See listing under *Reference.*)

DRESNER, SAMUEL H. *Prayer, Humility and Compassion.* Three dimensions of religious existence: man's relation to God, to himself, and to his fellow man. With woodcuts by Ilya Shor. Hartmore House, 1957, $4.95.

————————, and SIEGEL, SEYMOUR. *The Jewish Dietary Laws: Their Meaning for Our Time.* Also: *A Guide to Observance.* The basis of the dietary laws, the values they reflect and the details of their observance. United Synagogue, 1966, $1.50 paperback.

FRIEMAN, DONALD. *Milestones in the Life of the Jew.* Basic guide to belief and ritual, covering all personal religious events from birth to death. Bloch, 1965, $1.95 paperback.

GARFIEL, EVELYN. *The Service of the Heart: A Guide to the Jewish Prayer Book.* The significance of the prayers, the moral and ethical concepts of Judaism and the historical background of the prayer book. Wilshire, 1958, $3.00 paperback.

GASTER, THEORDORE. *Customs and Folkways of Jewish Life.* A modern folkloristic approach. William Sloane, 1955, $1.75 paperback.

—————————. *Festivals of the Jewish Year.* The fasts and holy days are examined as manifestations of a constantly evolving process. Peter Smith, 1962, $5.00 cloth; Morrow, 1971, $3.45 paperback.

GLATZER, NAHUM N., ed. *Language of Faith:* A selection from the most expressive Jewish prayers. Schocken, 1967, $4.95.

GOODMAN, PHILIP and HANNA. *The Jewish Marriage Anthology.* An illustrated anthology of stories, ritual, poetry and folklore. Jewish Publication Society, 1965, $6.00.

GOODMAN, PHILIP. *The Passover Anthology.* A collection of customs, music, folklore, recipes and stories as well as the historical background of Passover. Jewish Publication Society, 1961, $5.00.

—————————. *The Purim Anthology.* Purim in history, literature, art and music; Purim in many lands. Jewish Publication Society, 1952, $5.00.

—————————. *The Rosh Hashanah Anthology.* The significance of the new year as expressed in literature from the Bible to the present. Includes prayers with commentaries, parables, folklore, music, illustrations and program suggestions. Jewish Publication Society, 1970, $6.00.

—————————. *The Shavuot Anthology.* Selections from the major sources of Jewish literature and the writings of modern authors illuminate the festival. Jewish Publication Society, 1974, $7.95.

—————————. *Sukkot and Simhat Torah Anthology.* Includes historical and contemporary material on practically every level that will bring joy and knowledge to every household. Jewish Publication Society, 1973, $7.50.

——————————. *The Yom Kippur Anthology.* This book contains sections on Yom Kippur in the Bible, on writings in the Talmud and Midrash in medieval Jewish literature and in modern prose and poetry. Includes stories and poems for children with an account of how Yom Kippur has been celebrated all through the centuries by Jews of many lands. Jewish Publication Society, 1971, $7.50.

GREENBERG, SIDNEY, and SUGARMAN, S. ALLAN. *A Contemporary High Holy Day Service for Teenagers.* Looseleaf Mahzor meaningful and innovative. Prayer Book Press, 1970, $5.95.

GREENBERG, SIDNEY. *Likrat Shabbat.* $7.95. (See listing under *Prayer.*)

HERTZ, JOSEPH H. *Authorized Daily Prayerbook.* Richly annotated. English and Hebrew. Bloch, 1961, $12.50.

HESCHEL, ABRAHAM J. *Man's Quest for God: Studies in Prayer and Symbolism.* A valuable study of Jewish prayer and its role in the cosmos. Scribner's, 1954, $5.95.

——————————. *The Sabbath: Its Meaning for Modern Man.* A poetic evocation of the beauty of the traditional Sabbath. Farrar, Straus & Giroux, $2.95 paperback.

JACOBS, LOUIS. *Hasidic Prayer.* The motivating key to a spiritual world. Schocken, 1973, $10.00. (See listing under *Prayer.*)

KIEVAL, HERMAN. *The High Holidays.* A commentary on the prayer-book of Rosh Hashanah. Burning Bush Press, 1959, $5.00. (See listing under *Prayer.*)

LAMM, MAURICE. *The Jewish Way in Death and Mourning.* The laws and traditions are presented clearly. Jonathan David, 1969, $3.95 paperback.

LEVI, SHONIE, and KAPLAN, SYLVIA R. *Across the Threshold: A Guide for the Jewish Homemaker.* A practical introduction to Jewish observance. Illustrated. Schocken, 1970, $2.75 paperback.

MILLGRAM, ABRAHAM E. *Jewish Worship.* A widely acclaimed introduction to the nature of Jewish prayer. Jewish Publication Society, 1971, $8.50.

PETUCHOWSKI, JAKOB, ed. *Understanding Jewish Prayer.* A significant statement by a Reform rabbi. Ktav, 1972, $8.95.

RAPHAEL, CHAIM. *A Feast of History.* A complete Haggadah, with an excellent presentation of the history and themes of the Haggadah. Beautifully illustrated, rich with photographs. Simon and Schuster, 1972, $12.50.

RIEMER, JACK, ed. *Jewish Reflections on Death.* Out of the tradition come essays on the special problems posed by medical technology, modern society and interpersonal relations. Sensitive treatment of a difficult subject. Schocken Books, 1974, $7.95; $3.45 paperback.

ROCKLAND, MAE SHAFTER. *The Hanukkah Book.* The story, along with traditions, crafts, projects, recipes, and instructions for how to celebrate with zest, imagination and fun. Schocken, 1975, $10.00.

SCHAUSS, HAYYIM. *Guide to the Jewish Holidays: History and Observance.* Informative presentation. U.A.H.C., $1.95 paperback; Schocken, 1972, $2.95 paperback.

——————. *The Lifetime of a Jew: Throughout the Ages of Jewish History.* The traditional practices surrounding birth, maturation, courtship, marriage, and death are traced from Biblical times to the present. Illustrated, U.A.H.C., 1950, $6.50.

SPIRO, JACK D. *A Time to Mourn: Judaism and the Psychology of Bereavement.* The socio-religious aspects of the process of mourning as revealed in modern psychiatric research, as well as the Jewish theological background relating to the concept of death. Bloch, 1968, $4.95.

YERUSHALMI, YOSEF HAYIM. *Haggadah and History: A Panorama in Facsimile of Five Centuries of the Printed Haggadah.* An extensive survey of of the development of the Haggadah during the age of the printed word. Jewish Publication Society, 1975, $27.50.

THEOLOGY AND PHILOSOPHY

AGUS, JACOB B. *The Evolution of Jewish Thought.* A survey of significant philosophical and theological ideas in Judaism through the ages. Arno, 1959, $22.00.

—————————. *Modern Philosophies of Judaism.* Full-scale presentation of the thought of Hermann Cohen, Martin Buber, Mordecai Kaplan, and brief treatment of others. Fine analysis of Rosenzweig. Behrman House, 1941, $3.25 paperback.

—————————. *The Vision and the Way: An Interpretation of Jewish Ethics.* An interpretive anthology of Jewish ethical thought from the Bible to modern times. An important book. Frederick Ungar, 1966, $2.95 paperback.

ALTMANN, ALEXANDER; LEWY, HANS; and HEINEMANN, ISAAK. *Three Jewish Philosophers.* Selections from the major works of Philo, Saadya, and Judah Halevi—three important thinkers representing the encounter of Judaism with philosophy in three great centers and epochs of Jewish life. Atheneum, 1970, $4.95 paperback.

AMSEL, ABRAHAM. *Judaism and Psychology.* A theory of human behavior is presented within the framework of Judaism. Deals with dynamics of behavior, causes of mental illness, and therapeutic approaches. Feldheim, 1969, $5.95.

BAECK, LEO. *The Essence of Judaism.* A classic study of the enduring beliefs and values of Judaism. Schocken, 1948, $3.75.

BECKER, ERNEST. *The Denial of Death.* Psychological-philosophical synthesis of modern existence. Winner of the Pulitzer Prize. Macmillan, 1973, $2.95.

—————————. *Escape from Evil.* How evil caused by man stems from his efforts to deny his creatureliness and to overcome his insignificance. Macmillan, 1975, $9.95.

BERGMAN, SAMUEL HUGO. *Faith and Reason: An Introduction to Modern Jewish Thought.* Discussions of the works of Martin Buber, Hermann Cohen, A. D. Gordon, Zvi Yehudah Kook, Judah Magnes, and Franz Rosenzweig. Schocken Books, 1961, $1.75 paperback.

BERKOVITS, ELIEZER. *Crisis and Faith*. The crisis facing Judaism today and what our responses should be. Hebrew Publishing Co., 1975, $8.50.

——————. *Major Themes in Modern Philosophies of Judaism*. Critical analyses of the major themes in the thought of Hermann Cohen, Franz Rosenzweig, Martin Buber, Mordecai Kaplan, and Abraham Heschel. Ktav, 1974, $12.50 cloth; $4.95 paperback.

——————. *God, Man, and History*. Re-evaluation of man's relationship to God and his place in history. Jonathan David, 1959, $2.95 paperback.

BERNFELD, SIMON. *The Foundations of Jewish Ethics*. Ktav, 1929, $8.95.

BIRNBAUM, PHILIP, ed. *Karaite Studies*. Some of the most important monographs on the Karaites. Sepher Hermon Press, 1971, $12.50.

BOKSER, BEN ZION. *The Gifts of Life and Love*. Illustrated collection of prose and poetry to inspire, uplift and comfort. Hebrew Publishing Co., 1975, $5.00.

——————. *Pharisaic Judaism in Transition*. Arno, reprint of 1935 edition, $10.00.

BOROWITZ, EUGENE B. *How Can a Jew Speak of Faith Today?* How classical Jewish faith speaks to modern man. Westminster Press, 1969, $6.00.

——————. *A Layman's Introduction to Religious Existentialism*. An explanation and assessment of some important Jewish, Catholic and Protestant representatives of this school: Kierkegaard, Barth, Rosenzweig, Buber, Tillich. Dell Books, 1966, $1.95 paperback.

——————. *A New Jewish Theology in the Making*. An investigation of the possibilities for creating Jewish theology in this generation. Westminster Press, 1968, $6.50.

BUBER, MARTIN. *Between Man and Man*. Important collection of essays. Macmillan, 1965, $1.45 paperback.

——————. *Eclipse of God.* Essays on the understanding of God in modern philosophy. Harper & Row, 1952, $1.75 paperback.

——————. *I and Thou.* The new translation, prologue and notes by Walter Kaufmann are extremely helpful in clarifying Buber's thought. Scribner's, 1970, $2.45 paperback.

——————. *Israel and the World: Essays in a Time of Crisis.* An attempt to clarify the relation of certain aspects of Jewish thinking and living to contemporary intellectual movements and to analyze critically trends in Jewish life which tend to weaken the teachings of Israel. Schocken, 1963, $2.95 paperback.

COHEN, ARTHUR A. *The Natural and the Supernatural Jew.* On the particular relationship the Jew has with his destiny, the Covenant, the Jewish mission in history. Pantheon, $6.00; McGraw-Hill, 1963, $2.95 paperback.

COHEN, HERMANN. *Religion of Reason Out of the Sources of Judaism.* Magnum opus of the great Jewish philosopher. Ungar, 1971, $15.00. Also: *Reason and Hope: Sections from the Writings of Hermann Cohen,* translated and edited by Eva Jospe, B'nai B'rith & Viking Press, 1971, $6.50.

COLLINS, JAMES. *God in Modern Philsophy.* The vicissitudes of the idea of God in Western philosophy from the Renaissance to the present day. Regnery, $7.50.

The Condition of Jewish Belief: A Symposium, compiled by the editors of Commentary Magazine. Thirty-eight rabbis and theologians offer a contemporary restatement of the basic concepts of Judaism and discuss their relevance to the modern age.

ELIADE, MIRCEA. *Cosmos and History: The Myth of the Eternal Return.* A study of the nature of myth, the gulf separating mythical from Biblical religion, and the persistent tension between mythical and historical world views in Western civilization. Princeton Univ. Press, 1959, $2.45 paperback.

——————. *The Sacred and the Profane.* An eminent historian of religion discusses the importance of the sacred in human life and the universal symbols in which it is expressed. Harcourt Brace Jovanovich, 1968, $1.75 paperback.

EPSTEIN, ISIDORE. *Judaism: A Religious and Distinctive Way of Life.* Penguin, 1959, $1.75 paperback.

FACKENHEIM, EMIL C. *Encounter Between Judaism and Modern Philosophy.* Major work of contemporary philosophy and a challenge to future Jewish thought. Basic Books, 1972, $10.00.

————————. *God's Presence in History.* Jewish affirmations and philosophical reflections on history and the Holocaust. Harper & Row, 1972, $2.75 paperback.

————————. *Quest for Past and Future: Essays in Jewish Theology.* Judaism's relevance to the modern world examined in essays dealing with crucial religious questions. Beacon Press, 1970, $3.45 paperback.

FORCHEIMER, PAUL. *Living Judaism: The Mishneh of Aboth.* Complete annotated translations of Maimonides' Commentary on Pirkei Avot and his introduction to Helek, accompanied by several brief essays toward the formation of a truly Jewish modern philosophy. Feldheim, 1973, $10.00.

FOX, MARVIN, ed. *Modern Jewish Ethics: Theory and Practice.* A collection of original papers by many leading Jewish thinkers and theologians. Ohio State University, 1975, $12.50.

FRANKL, VIKTOR. *The Unconscious God: Psychotherapy and Theology.* Essential to man's humanity and the element that distinguishes him from the other animals is his awareness of God. Simon & Schuster, 1975, $6.95.

FRIEDMAN, MAURICE. *Martin Buber: The Life of Dialogue.* A good introduction to Buber's thought by one of his principal interpreters and translators. Harper & Row, 1960, $2.25 paperback.

GLATZER, NAHUM, N., ed. *The Essential Philo.* Presents the essential aspects of Philo's work. An introduction to Hellenistic Judaism, and the origins of Neoplatonist tradition. Schocken, 1971, $3.95 paperback.

GUTTMAN, JULIUS. *Philosophies of Judaism.* The history of Jewish philosophy from Biblical times to Franz Rosenzweig. Holt, Rinehart and Winston & Jewish Publication Society, 1964, $7.50; Schocken, 1964, $5.50 paperback.

HERBERG, WILL. *Judaism and Modern Man.* A strong, post-Holocaust assessment of Judaism. Atheneum, 1970, $3.95 paperback.

HESCHEL, ABRAHAM JOSHUA. *A Passion for Truth.* The ideas of Danish theologian Soren Kierkegaard (1813-1855) and the life of Rabbi Menachem Mendel of Kotzk (1787-1859). Farrar, Straus & Giroux, 1973, $8.95 cloth; $3.65 paperback.

—————————. *God in Search of Man: A Philosophy of Judaism.* An interpretation of God's relationship to man and of his concepts of revelation and deed in Jewish thought. Octagon, 1972, $14.50; Farrar, Straus & Giroux, 1976, $5.95 paperback.

—————————. *Man Is Not Alone: A Philosophy of Religion.* A discussion of the principles of faith and the challenge to modern man to understand himself and the world about him. Octagon, 1972, $11.75; Farrar, Straus & Giroux, 1976, $4.95 paperback. Other titles· *Who Is Man?* and *The Sabbath.*

HUSIK, ISAAC. *History of Medieval Jewish Philosophy.* Standard work. Atheneum, 1940, $4.95.

JACOBS, LOUIS. *Jewish Values.* Ethical and religious questions considered in the light of Jewish teachings in an attempt to bridge the gap between the teaching and their acceptance and application in Jewish life today. Hartmore House, 1970, $3.95.

—————————. *Faith.* Of the nature and meaning of faith—its way through reason, experience, tradition. Basic Books, 1968, Out of print.

——————. *The Principles of the Jewish Faith.* An extensive analysis of Maimonides' Principles. Basic Books, 1964, $9.50.

——————. *Theology in the Responsa.* A study of theological questions as they appear in Responsa literature, reflecting changing trends of thought and direction for practice. Routledge & Kegan Paul, 1975, $18.75.

——————. *A Jewish Theology.* A systematic presentation of the main themes of Jewish theology; the quest for Torah is basic. Behrman House, 1973, $12.50 cloth; $4.95 paperback.

KADUSHIN, MAX. *The Rabbinic Mind.* An exploration of the thought processes of the rabbis who shaped Judaism into a system of value concepts. Bloch, 1972, $4.95 paperback.

——————. *Worship and Ethics: A Study in Rabbinic Judaism.* On worship and its ethical concommitants. Bloch, 1964, $5.95. (See *Prayer.*)

KAUFMANN, WALTER. *Critique of Religion and Philosophy. Faith of a Heretic.* Two volumes offering astringent comment and sharp analyses on a wide range of problems. Harper & Row, 1972, $3.75 paperback.

KONVITZ, MILTON, ed. *Judaism and Human Rights.* Collection of essays mainly by contemporary scholars. B'nai Brith & Viking Press, 1972, $7.50.

LAMM, NORMAN, and WURZBURGER, WALTER S. *A Treasury of Tradition.* Anthology of essays first published in *Tradition* magazine. Hebrew Pub., 1967, $6.00.

MAIMONIDES, MOSES. *The Guide for the Perplexed.* Maimonides' principal philosophical work in which he attempts to demonstrate harmony between Biblical statements and philosophical principles. Translated by Shlomo Pines, University of Chicago Press, 1974, 2 volumes, $15.20 paperback. Translated by Maurice Friedlander, Hebrew Pub. Co., $9.50, one vol., cloth; Dover, 1956, $4.50 paperback.

——————. "Maimonides on Immortality and the Principles of Judaism." Translated by Arnold J. Wolf. *Judiasm,* Vol. 15, Nos. 1, 2, and 3. Maimonides' thirteen principles of faith are set forth as a condition for attaining immortality.
Also: *Maimonides Octocentennial Series,* Numbers I-IV. Essays on Maimonides by Ahad Ha'am, Alexander Marx, Chaim Tchernowitz, Isaac Husik. Arno Press, 1935, $9.00.
Also: *Maimonides Reader* by Isadore Twersky. An important analysis of the life and contributions of the philosopher. Behrman House, 1974, $12.50 cloth; $4.95 paperback.

MARTIN, BERNARD. *Great 20th Century Jewish Philosophers: A Reader in Jewish Existentialism.* Introductory essays and selections from Rosenzweig, Buber, and Russian genius Lev Shestov. Macmillan, 1969, $8.95 cloth; $2.45 paperback.

——————. *Contemporary Jewish Thought.* A collection of essays on Reform approaches to contemporary Judaism. Quadrangle, $5.95.

MENDELSSOHN, MOSES. *Selections from His Writings.* Edited and translated by Eva Jospe. B'nai B'rith, Viking Press, 1975, $10.00.

——————. *Jerusalem and Other Jewish Writings.* Translated by Alfred Jospe. The classic attempts to reconcile traditional Judaism with the ideas of the Enlightenment. Schocken Books, 1969, $5.95.

MILLGRAM, ABRAHAM E., ed. *Great Jewish Ideas.* Essays on the timeless ideas and ideals of Judaism made relevant for modern Jews, written by well-known scholars. B'nai B'rith Adult Education Department and Bloch Publishing Co., 1964, $5.95 cloth; $2.95 paperback.

MINKIN, JACOB S. *The World of Moses Maimonides.* An introduction to the life and writings of the great philosopher with selections from his writings. Thomas Yoseloff, 1957, $5.95. Out of print.

MOURANT, JOHN A., ed. *Readings in the Philosophy of Religion.* Selections from classical philosophers on the topics of God, mysticism, faith, evil, and eschatology. Apollo Eds., $3.25 paperback.

THEOLOGY AND PHILOSOPHY

NEUSNER, JACOB, ed. *Understanding Jewish Theology.* Includes a wide range of contemporary thinkers. A good introduction, Ktav, 1973, $7.95; $4.95 paperback.

—————————. *The Way of Torah: An Introduction to Judaism.* A compact introduction to Jewish thought and history and observance. Dickenson, 1970, $3.95 paperback.

NOVECK, SIMON, ed. *Great Jewish Thinkers of the 20th Century. Contemporary Jewish Thought: A Reader.* One volume contains the biographies, the other, writings of these important thinkers. B'nai B'rith Adult Education Department and Bloch, 1963, $5.95 cloth; $2.95 paperback.

OLIVER, ROY. *The Wanderer and the Way: The Hebrew Tradition in the Writings of Martin Buber.* The writer develops his portrait by positing several Biblical archetypes and the growth of Buber's response to them, from Hasidic sources through I-Thou philosophy. Cornell Univ. Press, 1968, $4.95.

OTTO, RUDOLPH. *The Idea of the Holy.* Classic study of the non-rational core of religion. Oxford Univ., 1950, $7.50.

OUTKA, GENE, and REEDER, JOHN P., Jr. *Religion and Morality.* Anchor Books, 1973, $4.95 paperback.

RAWIDOWICZ, SIMON. *Studies in Jewish Thought.* Edited by Nahum N. Glatzer; preface by Abram L. Sachar. Essays on Saadia Gaon, Maimonides, Moses Mendelssohn, and Rabbi Nahman Krochmal, and the philosophy of Jewish history. Jewish Publication Society, $6.95.

RIEMER, JACK, ed. *Jewish Reflections on Death.* Collection of essays by famous writers, philosophers and religious leaders on Judaism's attitudes towards death. Contributors: Elie Weisel, Abraham Heschel, Hans J. Morgenthau, Hayim Greenberg, and Milton Steinberg. Schocken, 1974, $7.95; $3.45 paperback.

ROSENBLOOM, NOAH H. *Luzzatto's Ethico-Psychological Interpretation of*

Judaism. A study of religious philosophy. Yeshiva University Press, Studies in Torah Judaism, No. 7. Bloch, 1965, $4.00.

ROSENZWEIG, FRANZ. *On Jewish Learning.* Edited by Nahum Glatzer. Contains the important essay, "The Builders: Concerning the Law," and an exchange of letters with Buber on revelation and law. Schocken Books, 1955, $1.34 paperback. Out of print.

ROTENSTREICH, NATAN. *Jewish Philosophy in Modern Times: From Mendelssohn to Rosenzweig.* Philosophical studies of several 18th, 19th and 20th century figures in Jewish philosophy. Holt, Rinehart and Winston, 1968, $6.50.

RUDAVSKY, DAVID. *Modern Jewish Religious Movements: A History of Emancipation and Adjustment.* The origins, growth and evolution of the ideologies of the contemporary religious alignments as they have arisen and developed in Europe and America. Behrman House, 1972, $3.95 paperback.

SCHILPP, PAUL ARTHUR, and FRIEDMAN, MAURICE, eds. *The Philosophy of Martin Buber.* A Critical analysis and evaluation by philosophers and scholars. Open Court, 1967, $15.00.

SCHWARTZ, CHARLES and BERTIE G. *A Modern Interpretation of Judaism: Faith Through Reason.* A succinct presentation of the essence of Judaism, its principles and ideals and th reasoning underlying them. Schocken, 1976, $3.95.

SILVER, DANIEL JEREMY, ed. *Judaism and Ethics.* Ktav, 1970, 12.50.

SIMON, LEON, ed. *Ahad Ha'am: Selected Essays.* Atheneum, 1970, $3.95 paperback.

SMART, NINIAN. *The Phenomenon of Religion.* A concept of religion described from the point of view of descriptive phenomenology. Seabury, 1973, $6.95.

STEINBERG, MILTON. *Anatomy of Faith: The Theological Essays of Milton*

THEOLOGY AND PHILOSOPHY

STEINBERG, MILTON. *Anatomy of Faith: The Theological Essays of Milton Steinberg.* Edited by Arthur A. Cohen. Theological papers of a Conservative thinker and leader, including discussions of modern theological problems and trends. Harcourt Brace Jovanovich, 1960, $4.95.

——————————. *Basic Judaism.* A concise introduction to Jewish beliefs and practices. Harcourt Brace Jovanovich, 1960, $4.95; $1.65 paperback.

STITSKIN, LEON D., ed. *Studies in Judaica in Honor of Dr. Samuel Belkin.* A Festschrift containing some excellent monographs. Originally published in Yeshiva University Monographs. Ktav, 1974, $15.00.

——————————. *Studies in Torah Judaism.* (See listing under *Prayer.*)

TILLICH, PAUL. *Dynamics of Faith.* Definitions and distinctions for understanding the meaning of religious faith. Harper & Row, 1957, $1.25.

URY, ZALMAN F. *The Musar Movement.* A quest for excellence in character education. Yeshiva University Press, Studies in Torah Judaism, No. 12, 1970, $3.25.

VAN DER LEEUW, GERARDUS. *Religion in Essence and Development.* A systematic study of the nature, varieties and basic concepts of religion. Harper & Row, 2 volumes, $2.95 each, paperback.

WAXMAN, MEYER. *Judaism: Religion and Ethics.* The ethical and moral values, ritual and social institutions which make up the traditional Jewish way of life. A. S. Barnes, 1958, $6.95.

WAXMAN, MORDECAI. *Tradition and Change.* A source book of essays and addresses by leaders of the Conservative movement, indicating distinctive approaches to various practical issues. Burning Bush Press, 1958, $7.00.

AUTHOR INDEX

AUTHOR INDEX

AUTHOR INDEX

AUTHOR INDEX

AUTHOR INDEX

S

AUTHOR INDEX

TITLE INDEX

TITLE INDEX

TITLE INDEX

TITLE INDEX

TITLE INDEX

TITLE INDEX

TITLE INDEX

TITLE INDEX

TITLE INDEX

THE ATID BIBLIOGRAPHY was designed by Alvin Schultzberg. Cover by Laura Karp. Production supervision by The Town House Press, Spring Valley, New York.